HERBERT SPENCER

Masters of Social Theory
Volume 1

MASTERS OF SOCIAL THEORY

Series Editor:

Jonathan H. Turner, *University of California, Riverside*

This new series of short volumes presents prominent social theorists of the nineteenth and twentieth centuries. Current theory in sociology involves analysis of these early thinkers' work, which attests to their enduring significance. However, secondary analysis of their work is often hurried in larger undergraduate texts or presented in long scholarly portraits.

Our attempt is to provide both scholarly analysis and also to summarize the basic, core idea of the individual master. Our goal is to offer both a short scholarly reference work and individual texts for undergraduate and graduate students.

Forthcoming volumes and their authors include the following:

Randall Collins, *University of California, Riverside*   MAX WEBER
Charles H. Powers, *Indiana University*   VILFREDO PARETO
Robert Alun Jones, *University of Illinois*   EMILE DURKHEIM
John D. Baldwin, *University of California,*
Santa Barbara   GEORGE HERBERT MEAD
Richard P. Appelbaum, *University of California,*
Santa Barbara   KARL MARX

HERBERT SPENCER

A Renewed Appreciation

Jonathan H. Turner

Masters of Social Theory
Volume 1

Cover photo: Culver Pictures

SAGE PUBLICATIONS Beverly Hills London New Delhi

For information address:

SAGE Publications, Inc.
275 South Beverly Drive
Beverly Hills, California 90212

SAGE Publications India Pvt. Ltd. SAGE Publications Ltd
M-32 Market   28 Banner Street
Greater Kailash I   London EC1Y 8QE
New Delhi 110 048 India   England

Printed in the United States of America

Library of Congress Cataloging in Publication Data

Turner, Jonathan H.
  Herbert Spencer: a renewed appreciation

  (Masters of social theory)
  Includes index.
  1. Spencer, Herbert, 1820-1903. 2. Sociology.
I. Title. II. Series.
HM22.G8S775   1985   301′.092′4   84-24969
ISBN   0-8039-2244-2
ISBN   0-8039-2426-7 (pbk.)

FIRST PRINTING

CONTENTS

Preface   7

1   Herbert Spencer: The Enigma and Stigma   9

The Enigmatic Spencer   11
The Stigmatized Spencer   13
Toward a Revaluation of Spencer   15

2   The Earlier Rules of the Sociological Method   16

Is Social Science Possible?   18
The Nature of Social Science   20
Methodological Dilemmas of Sociology   22
Resolving Research Dilemmas   26

3   The First General Systems Theorist   30

The Rise and Fall of General Systems Theory   30
Spencer's "First Principles"   32
Spencer's General Systems Theory   43

4   The First Functionalist   49

The Beginning and End of Analytical Functionalism   49
Principles of Sociology, Part I:
    On Preliminary Considerations   52
Principles of Sociology, Part II:
    Structuring and Function   55

5   The Analytical Models and Abstract Principles   63

Spencer as a Theorist   63
The Overall Analytical Model   65
Models and Principles of System Growth
    and Differentiation   69
Models and Principles of Political Dialectics   79
The Theoretical Legacy and the Lost Promise   82

6   Spencer's Human Relations Area Files   **85**

Spencer's Descriptive Model of Societal Evolution   86
Spencer's Descriptive Model of Political Dialectics   92
Spencer's Human Relations Area Files   95
The Lost Legacy: Summary and Preview   104

**7   The Creation of Society: Spencer on
       Domestic Institutions**   **106**

Spencer on Institutional Analysis in General   106
Spencer on Domestic Institutions   109
Conclusion   115

8   The Micro Basis of Society: Spencer on Ceremony   **116**

The Pre- and Subinstitutional   116
Components of Ceremony   117
Conclusions   121

9   Power and Class: Spencer on Political Institutions   **123**

The Elements of Spencer's Political Sociology   124
The Evolution of Government   126
Political Structuring and Evolution   128
Political Evolution and Class Systems   132
Conclusions   134

**10 The Elementary and Complex Forms of Religious Life:
       Spencer on Ecclesiastical Institutions**   **136**

The Functional and Structural Basis of Religion   136
The Origins of Religion   137
The Evolution of Religion   138
Conclusion   141

**11 Economy and Society:
       Spencer on Industrial Institutions**   **142**

Economic Production and Distribution   143
Capital Formation   146
The Organization of Labor   147
Conclusion   153

Author Index   **155**

Subject Index   **156**

About the Author   **160**

Preface

I have written these pages because I am distressed, even angry, about how contemporary social theorists have treated Herbert Spencer. At a time when social theorists genuflect at the sacred works of St. Marx, St. Durkheim, and St. Weber, we spit on the grave of Spencer because he held a moral philosophy repugnant to the political biases of many contemporary theorists. I share these biases, but they should not blind all of us to a simple fact: Spencer's sociology and his moral philosophy are written in separate places and are worlds apart. One finds far less moralizing in Spencer's sociology than that of either Durkheim or Marx; and yet, we continue to ignore Spencer.

Ordinarily, I am not an advocate of social theory that is little more than hero worship of the first masters. Indeed, I feel that social theorists spend far too much time reading and re-analyzing the canonized fathers to the detriment of theory development and cumulation. We stand in the shadows of Marx, Weber, and Durkheim rather than on their shoulders. So it can be asked legitimately: Why write about a sociological theorist who, to say the least, has not cast a very wide shadow on contemporary sociology? The answer, I must confess, is my sense of injustice over how Spencer has been treated. There are so many misconceptions about Spencer that someone needs to set the record straight.

Moreover, Spencer's ideas are still useful and relevant. And as I will try to demonstrate, our ignorance of what Spencer really said has hurt the cumulation of sociological knowledge. For we have had to rediscover many of Spencer's theoretical ideas, his methodological precepts, and his empirical generalizations. We do not recognize this fact, because we are so ignorant of Spencer's work, but the unknowing rediscovery of Spencer over the last one hundred years represents an enormous waste of our intellectual energies.

I am not a historian of ideas, so this is not a book on the time and context of Spencer. Rather, it is a book about what is still useful and interesting in Spencer's sociology. I am admittedly a "presentist," in Robert Alum Jones's words, and proud of it. I make no apologies for not doing history. And so, as you read these pages, be prepared for a summary and analysis of Spencer's work, not the "mood of the times" or some such thing. I am concerned only with his relevance for contemporary sociology.

Spencer was a fascinating intellectual and a profound thinker. I can only hope that sociology's collective bigotry against him can be overcome. It is to doing so that I dedicate these pages.

Laguna Beach, California   —*Jonathan H. Turner*

1

Herbert Spencer

The Enigma and Stigma

Herbert Spencer was born in 1820 in Derby, England.[1] Until the age of thirteen, he was tutored by his father at home; and at thirteen, he continued his private education with his uncle at Bath. Although his father had attended Cambridge, Spencer felt himself unqualified to attend college, and so in 1837, he sought to use his mathematical and scientific training by becoming an engineer for the London and Birmingham Railway. In 1841, when the railway was completed, he returned to Derby; and in the next few years, he wrote several articles in the radical press and numerous letters to the editor of a dissenting paper, *The Nonconformist,* in which he argued for limitations on the power and sphere of government. Such ideas were radical in their time; it is only through our present political eyeglasses that they are viewed as conservative, indeed even "right wing."

In 1848, after several years of operating on the fringes of radical politics and journalism as a writer, Spencer landed a stable position as a subeditor for the London *Economist.* From this point on, Spencer's career as an intellectual and scholar accelerated. In 1851, he published

---

1. This brief biographical portrayal is extracted from Lewis A. Coser's *Masters of Sociological Thought* (New York: Harcourt Brace Jovanovich, 1971)—one of the few texts to treat Spencer accurately and fairly.

Social Statics[2] which was to haunt him for the rest of his career and to color our retrospective view of Spencer. In this work, Spencer championed the cause of laissez-faire and the need for restrictions on the scope of government. The book was well received and opened doors to the intellectual community, but it was also to become a burden for Spencer as he sought to write more scientific works.

In 1853, his uncle died and left him a considerable inheritance, which prompted Spencer to quit his job as an editor and assume the life of a private scholar. He was a lifelong bachelor, living a reclusive life in modest lodgings. Over the years, he became highly neurotic, suffering extreme insomnia and depression. Yet, even as he became increasingly unable to cope with the outside world, Spencer was prolific. In 1854, he published *Principles of Psychology,*[3] which, despite some indifferent reviews, was used as a text at Harvard and Cambridge. In 1862, he published *First Principles,*[4] the opening statement of his grand "Synthetic Philosophy" that was to unify all sciences under a common set of abstract principles. Between 1864 and 1867, he published the several volumes of his *Principles of Biology.*[5] But it was not until 1873 that he published his first sociological work, *The Study of Sociology.*[6] And in 1874, the first installments of *The Principles of Sociology*[7] were published; however, the last portions of *The Principles of Sociology* were not published until 1896. Only from 1873 to 1896, then, did Spencer devote his energies to sociological analysis, and even then he was concurrently publishing installments of his *Principles of Ethics,*[8] which restated the then liberal (now conservative) ideology of his first book, *Social Statics.* Spencer was thus a sociologist for only two decades.

2. Herbert Spencer, *Social Statics; Or the Conditions Essential to Human Happiness Specified, and First of Them Developed* (New York: Appleton, 1888, originally published in 1852).

3. Herbert Spencer, *The Principles of Psychology,* two volumes (New York: Appleton, 1898, originally published in 1851).

4. Herbert Spencer, *First Principles* (New York: A. L. Burt, 1880, originally published in 1862).

5. Herbert Spencer, *The Principles of Biology,* two volumes (New York: Appleton, 1897, originally published between 1864 and 1867).

6. Herbert Spencer, *The Study of Sociology* (London: Kegan, Paul, Trench, 1873).

7. Herbert Spencer, *Principles of Sociology,* three volumes (New York: Appleton, 1898, originally published between 1874 and 1896). Note that here and elsewhere I have shortened the title of this work. Most portions of this work were first published as serialized articles in popular science magazines and only later complied into separate volumes.

8. Herbert Spencer, *The Principles of Ethics,* two volumes (New York: Appleton, 1904, originally published between 1875-1896).

Even if Spencer had been an emotionally healthy person, which he was not, he would have been considered enormously productive. Moreover, he was one of the most widely read scholars of the last century. His published books sold close to 400,000 copies, and when we consider that most of them first appeared as serialized articles in popular science magazines, his audience in both the literate lay public and scientific community was immense. Yet, before his death in 1903, Spencer felt that he had never been fully appreciated, despite his wide following over the previous fifty years. In a sense he was right, for by the second decade of this century, Spencerian sociology was lost to most practicing social scientists.

I have opened this book with a brief review of Spencer's intellectual biography because it helps place into context my purpose in this short chapter: (a) to explain why Spencer remains an enigma to contemporary sociologists who devote much of their intellectual and emotional energy to discovering ever more about Spencer's approximate contemporaries: Karl Marx, Max Weber, Émile Durkheim, Georg Simmel, and others; and (b) to understand why Spencer and Spencerian sociology have become so stigmatized.

THE ENIGMATIC SPENCER

Contemporary sociologists, even social theorists, do not seem well acquainted with Spencer or his sociological works. True, he is usually mentioned in introductory texts as one of the first sociologists, and he is always given coverage in history of sociological theory courses. Occasionally one catches a reference to him. But in comparison with Marx, Weber, and Durkheim, Spencer and his work remain only vaguely familiar. He is acknowledged to have developed functional analysis—always to his discredit. We remember that he employed organic analogies, comparing societies and biological organisms. We recall that he was an evolutionist, tracing the development of societies from simple to complex. We never forget that he coined the phrase, "survival of the fittest," and was an apologist for the doctrine of laissez-faire. We have even defined him as a social Darwinist, even though a more accurate view would be to see Darwin as a biological Spencerian.[9] At any rate, these stereotypical views of Spencer exhaust most sociologists' knowledge of Spencer.[10] All of the elements in this

9. As Spencer coined this phrase "survival of the fittest," ten years prior to the publication of *On the Origin of Species*.

10. There are, of course, a number of prominent exceptions. See, for example, Robert G. Perrin, "Herbert Spencer's Four Theories of Social Evolution," *The American Jour-*

stereotype contribute to the stigmatization of Spencer, as I will discuss shortly. But why do we know so little about one of our past giants? Why do we have only vague stereotypical knowledge of his work?

Part of the answer to these questions resides in Spencer's intellectual style. First, he did not have an academic degree or an academic position. Thus he never taught students who could carry on his work. Indeed, he tended to hire full-fledged academics to do research for him, but he never taught younger students who would defend his ideas. Second, he was a very private person who did not like to give public lectures or to interact with people other than his scientific and literary friends at various clubs in London. Thus he was never known personally—except by a few—beyond what he published; and so, he had few loyal defenders when his ideas came under attack.

Third, Spencer was not a traditional scholar. He did not read very much; rather, he listened to and questioned some of the leading scientists of his time in his daily afternoon visits to various clubs in London. He absorbed ideas and used them in developing his Synthetic Philosophy, but he did not footnote extensively or seem aware of many prominent thinkers. He was not scholastic, to say the least, and in a traditional academic world this is a great sin. Indeed, it is important in academia to appear more scholarly than smart. As a result, many academics would not accept his ideas, despite their brilliance, and as a consequence they were not passed on to students.

Fourth, Spencer was a generalist in an age when the intellectual world was becoming highly specialized. He was a philosopher, psychologist, biologist, sociologist, and social commentator in an era when a scholar was supposed to pursue a narrow specialty within only one of these general fields. His ideas would always seem too general and imprecise for those who could not see the tree for the pine needle, to say nothing of the forest for the trees.

And thus, although most scholars and many laypersons have heard the name—Herbert Spencer—and have some vague stereotypes about his work, he remains a mystery. He is prominent and obscure at the same time. We know a little about him, but not much. And what we do know about his work has served to stigmatize him and anyone who would dare to take his work seriously.

nal of Sociology 81 (May, 1976), pp. 1339-1359; Coser, Masters of Sociological Thought; Stanislav Andreski, Herbert Spencer: Structure, Function and Evolution (New York: Joseph, 1971); J.D.Y. Peel, ed., "Introduction" to Herbert Spencer on Evolution (Chicago: University of Chicago Press, 1972); Robert L. Carneiro, ed., "Introduction" to The Evolution of Society (Chicago: University of Chicago Press, 1967). Even these otherwise excellent works, however, overemphasize the stereotyped portions of Spencer's work.

THE STIGMATIZED SPENCER

Late in his life,[11] Spencer complained bitterly that too much attention had been paid to his first work, *Social Statics*[12] where his famous "survival of the fittest" argument is used to promote a social system based upon free markets and a recessive government. Lost in the rhetoric of this immature work, he felt, were his volumes on biology, psychology, and sociology. To a degree, he was correct in that his moral philosophy has tended to obscure an objective and dispassionate assessment of his scientific work. But he also brought much of this grief on himself, because he continued to argue in his less scientific works for this extreme laissez-faire position. Indeed, his 1896 work, *Principles of Ethics,*[13] repeats the thesis of his early social commentary.

Even more than Spencer could have realized, his sociology has been ignored because of this moral philosophy. Today such a philosophy is politically conservative—even right wing—whereas contemporary sociology is decidedly liberal, radical, and collectivist. Although I share these biases to an extent, nonetheless, they are prejudices that have blinded us to the merits of Spencer's scientific work. We are simply unwilling to read anyone who is, by today's inverted political yardstick, conservative (of course, Spencer was a radical in his time). The tragedy here is that Spencer's scientific works are surprisingly devoid of his ideology. I am not asserting that his sociology was not influenced by his ideology; I am only pointing to the fact that there are far fewer ideological tracks in his work than in Durkheim's, Weber's, and Marx's works. Moreover, to the extent that Spencer's sociology was influenced by his ideological commitments, it represents a needed corrective to Marx, Weber, and Durkheim, who were all in different ways naively collectivist. Spencer's work is refreshing in its willingness to address sociologically many issues that Marx and Durkheim simply did not want to confront.

But the damage to Spencer has already been done. We worship the naive collectivism of Marx and Durkheim as well as the excessive pessimism of Weber while we stigmatize Spencer's analysis. However, a careful reading of Spencer would, I think, surprise most sociologists because his sociology is remarkably evenhanded and dispassionate. Moreover, as we will come to see in the chapters to follow, his sociology is anything but conservative.

11. Herbert Spencer, *An Autobiography,* two volumes (New York: Appleton, 1904).
12. See note 2.
13. See note 8.

Another reason for the stigma on Spencer's work can be found in its functionalism. Curiously, we do not stigmatize Durkheim, Radcliffe-Brown, and even Marx for their functionalism,[14] but we heap abuse on Spencer for advocating a functional mode of analysis. Actually, Spencer's functionalism—that is, structures exist because they meet the needs or survival requisites of a society—is far less intrusive than Durkheim's.[15] Moreover, unlike modern functionalists, Spencer's analysis is often a legitimate mode of explanation because it is used as a shorthand way to express "selection pressures" in historical societies for certain kinds of structures (much as it is in biology). But what is even more surprising in a careful reading of Spencer is that the functional statements are almost always superfluous to the more general analytical point. And thus it is unfair to stigmatize Spencer more than most other nineteenth-century thinkers for the functional elements in their work.

Yet another source of stigma on Spencer is his evolutionism. Most secondary portrayals of Spencer see him as a naive, ethnocentric, unilineal evolutionist who saw societies as marching toward the Anglo-Saxon ideal. Nothing could be further from the truth. Spencer uses an evolutionary perspective in a highly sophisticated way. It is anything but naive, unilineal, or ethnocentric. Indeed, compared to Marx's and Durkheim's utopias, Spencer is downright cold-hearted, pessimistic, and even anarchistic. As I will demonstrate in later chapters, we would do well to examine Spencer's evolutionary thinking before we stigmitize him as being more flagrant and naive than Marx and Durkheim.

A final reason for the stigma on Spencer's work is that he thought big. He always looked at the big picture in the sense of comparing simple and complex systems and in the commitment to examining the areas of isomorphism among the various sciences. Such an approach is always viewed suspiciously in a discipline that has splintered its practitioners into narrow specialties. Moreover, with the demise of Parsonian grand theory, anything that even looks global is condemned as mere armchair, grand theory. What critics fail to appreciate is that Spencer provided literally thousands of pages of ethnographic data to

14. See Alexandra Maryanski's and my book *Functionalism* (Menlo Park, CA: Benjamin-Cummings, 1978) for a review of this orientation and specific scholars' version of it.

15. For example, compare Spencer's *The Study of Sociology* and *Principles of Sociology* with Émile Durkheim's *The Rules of the Sociological Method* (New York: Free Press, 1938, originally published in 1895) and *The Division of Labor in Society* (New York: Free Press, 1947, originally published in 1893) to see just who is more functional.

illustrate his points. And more important, his theoretical ideas are always statements of covariance among abstractly defined concepts. Parsonian theory was bad not because it was grand or abstract; rather, its problems resided in the fact that it was not theory but typology. We should not, therefore, condemn Spencer for Parson's errors.

TOWARD A REVALUATION OF SPENCER

In sum, I think that sociology has been unfair to Spencer. We have ignored his work, which—as I hope to demonstrate—is filled with interesting and important ideas. And we have stigmatized Spencer to such a degree that no one would dare claim that he or she was a Spencerian in an era when social theorists fall all over themselves proclaiming that they are Marxians, Weberians, Durkheimians, and Meadians.

My belief is that we should be none of these "ians," because in making such proclamations, we admit to putting intellectual blinders on ourselves. Even with the phrase "neo-"—as in neo-Weberian—we confess to a certain degree of close-mindedness. Thus in writing these pages, I am not coming out of an intellectual closet and announcing that I am a Spencerian. My goal is only to right what I believe has been a great wrong in sociology and to give Spencer his due. And as with all historical figures, we should extract what is useful in their work and then move on, relegating scholars of the past to the footnotes of our own creative efforts. The pages to follow can thus be seen as my attempt to give us a more appreciative view of what we footnote when we cite Spencer.

2

The Earlier Rules
of the Sociological Method

In the early 1830s,[1] Auguste Comte laid the foundation for sociological methods. He argued that the collection of data must be directed toward testing theories and that, without being informed by theory, such collection is a "great hindrance" to sociology:[2]

> The next great hindrance to the use of observation is the empiricism which is introduced into it by those who, in the name of impartiality, would interdict the use of any theory whatever. No other dogma could by more thoroughly irreconcilable with the spirit of the positive philosophy.

Ironically, the very "raw empiricism" that Comte abhorred is identified today with "positivism."[3] Comte is, no doubt, turning in his grave over what has become of positivistic sociology. Nevertheless, as is well known, Comte outlined four methods for collecting data

1. Auguste Comte, *System of Positive Philosophy* (Paris: Bachelier, 1830-1842). References to follow are to the 1896 edition of Harriet Martineau's translation and condensation of the original work, *The Positive Philosophy of Auguste Comte,* Volumes 1, 2, and 3 (London: George Bell and Sons, 1896).

2. Comte, *Positive Philosophy,* p. 242 in Volume 2.

3. Indeed, there is a further irony in that Comte's preferred title for our discipline, "social physics," had to be abandoned because the Belgian statistician Adolphe Quetelet had already used this label to develop a statistical approach to sociology.

in order to test theories: observation, experimentation, comparison, and historical analysis.[4]

In his discussion of these approaches can be found the beginnings of a functional method. That is, data collection should ask these questions: What does a set of empirical processes do for the larger social whole? How is the social whole maintained or changed by social pressures? Comte never developed this functionalism into an explicit method, but over six decades later, Émile Durkheim did.

With the 1895 publication of his *The Rules of the Sociological Method*,[5] Durkheim codified two elements of sociological methods: the search for causes and functions. The observation of a "social fact" must involve efforts to interpret it in terms of "the efficient cause which produces it and the function it fulfills."[6] In making this assertion, Durkheim ignored Comte's advice to avoid excessive concern with first (causal) and final causes (functions).[7] But Durkheim's rules of the sociological method became the guiding principles of twentieth-century sociological analysis. For sociology has been engaged in a functional[8] and causal orgy for most of this century.[9] We are just now shedding the last remains of functional analysis, and we are still in the grasp of "causal mania" where the goal of theory and research is to explain the "causes" of some phenomenon.

I have emphasized this French tradition because it is the one that has dominated our sociological imaginations. True, we do not assign Comte's *Course of Positive Philosophy* or Durkheim's *The Rules of the Sociological Methods* to students in methods classes, but these works are still the underlying inspiration for much of what we do—even if most practitioners remain unaware of this fact. Between Comte's and Durkheim's pronouncements, Herbert Spencer wrote *The Study of Sociology*.[10] In virtually every respect, this is a work vastly superior

4. Comte, *Positive Philosophy,* pp. 217-246 in Volume 2.

5. Émile Durkheim, *The Rules of The Sociological Method* (New York: Free Press, 1938, originally published in 1895).

6. Ibid., p. 95.

7. As Comte, *Positive Philosophy,* pp. 5-6, noted, "our business is—seeing how vain is any search into what are called *causes,* whether first or final—to pursue an accurate discovery of . . . Laws, with a view to reducing them to the smallest possible number."

8. For a review, see Alexandra Maryanski's and my book *Functionalism* (Menlo Park: Benjamin-Cummings, 1979).

9. For a critique of "causal sociology," see David and Judith Willer, *Systematic Empiricism: Critique of a Pseudoscience* (Englewood Cliffs, NJ: Prentice-Hall, 1973).

10. Herbert Spencer, *The Study of Sociology* (London: Kegan Paul, Trench, 1873).

to either Comte's or Durkheim's methodological proclamations. And yet it is virtually ignored. Moreover, it is a book that could be assigned to undergraduates who would learn about the inherent dilemmas of conducting sociological research. It is literate and interesting, especially as it was published in both England and the United States in *Contemporary Review* and *Popular Science Monthly* as serialized articles in 1872. In 1873, it was published as a book in the publisher's "international scientific series."

My goal in this chapter is to dust off this work, that was written over twenty years before Durkheim's *Rules,* and to argue that this was by far the best methodological treatise in sociology of the last century. In fact, it still seems relevant to the present day, whereas Durkheim's *Rules* seems a bit archaic.

IS SOCIAL SCIENCE POSSIBLE?

Spencer opens *The Study of Sociology* by addressing an issue that still divides sociology: Can sociology and social science in general be "true" sciences? Can sociology be like the other natural sciences? Spencer's answer is "yes" to both questions; and his line of argument is still relevant.[11]

He begins by noting a common contradiction of laypersons. On the one hand, they resist the idea that the social world reveals invariant and lawlike regularities, whereas on the other, they make pronouncements and assertions about what will and should occur as if there were lawful regularities in the social world. One cannot have it both ways, Spencer argues. If there are no laws of human organization, then legislators, speculators, opinion makers, commentators, and others who comment upon and act in the world should "draw lots" or "toss coins." For if there are no lawful regularities in human organization,

> government and legislation are absurd. Acts of Parliament may, as well. . .be made to depend upon the drawing of lots or the tossing of a coin; or rather, there may as well be none at all: social sequences having no ascertainable order, no effect can be counted upon—everything is chaotic.[12]

11. Ibid., Chapters 1 and 2.
12. Ibid., pp. 46-47.

Today there is a kind of intellectual anarchism in sociology. There are many who refuse to believe that the social world reveals regularities that can be understood and stated in lawlike ways. If such is the case, sociology is unnecessary, and those who do not believe that the world reveals regularities should retire or write opinion columns for newspapers. Moreover, if such advice seems too extreme, then it is likely that even the anarchistic hold "folk conceptions" of social regularities. Indeed, I have always found that intellectual anarchists are rarely reluctant to offer opinions on what the nature of the world is and what its basic processes are. And thus although they may explicitly reject the view that there are invariant laws of social organization, they implicitly assert what these laws are—or should be—about. As Spencer would note, one cannot have it both ways; and if we wish to assert "what is" and "what should be" in the world, then we should seek to discover those laws of social organization that govern those processes about which we have strong opinions. And so, if there is

> natural causation, then the combination of forces by which every combination of effects is produced, produces that combination of effects in conformity with the laws of the forces. And if so, it behooves us to use all diligence in ascertaining what the forces are, what are their laws, and what are the ways in which they co-operate.[13]

To those who argue that such laws can never be like those of the "exact sciences"—a fact that removes sociology from science—Spencer reminds us that only portions of any science are "exact"; and what is exact at one time is subject to refutation at another as new data or better theory are brought to bear. Moreover, some of the most insightful theories of science are not stated mathematically or quantitatively, and yet, this fact does not disqualify them as a science. Indeed, when scientists must work in the natural empirical world, as opposed to artificial experiments, it becomes extremely difficult to be exact. Indeed, in sciences studying these orders of phenomena, their basic processes are produced by

> factors so numerous and so hard to measure, that to develop our knowledge of their relations into the quantitative form will be extremely difficult, if not impossible. But these orders of phenomena are not therefore excluded from the conception of Science. In Geology, in Biology, and

13. Ibid., p. 47.

> Psychology, most of the prevision are qualitative only. . . . Nevertheless
> we unhesitatingly class these previsions as scientific. It is thus with
> Sociology.[14]

Although the interaction effects of variables in natural empirical systems
make our task more difficult and less amenable to mathematical
precision, we can still uncover basic laws of many social phenomena.
Some events may resist our efforts, but "so far as there can be
generalization, and so far as there can be interpretation based on
it, so far can there be Science."[15] Because sociologists and laypersons
alike generalize and interpret, they acknowledge that sociology as
a science can exist. For

> whoever expresses political opinions—whoever asserts that such or such
> public arrangements will be beneficial or detrimental, tacitly expresses
> belief in a Social Science; for he asserts, by implication, that there is
> a natural sequence among social actions, and that as the sequence is
> natural results may be foreseen.[16]

These opening arguments are, I feel, far more compelling than
Durkheim's polemics in *Rules* about "social facts." Yet, we continue
to ignore them and cite Durkheim as the great defender of sociology
in a hostile intellectual world. Moreover, Spencer's broad outline of
what "structural sociology" should do is, once again, more interesting
than Durkheim's caveats about society as emergent reality *sui generis.*
Let me now turn to Spencer's view about the nature of social science.

THE NATURE OF SOCIAL SCIENCE

As is well known, Spencer's mode of sociological analysis drew from
his previously published *Principles of Biology.*[17] As a result, he saw
sociology as involving an emphasis on "morphology and physiology"
of what he was later to call "super-organic" bodies (that is, organized relations among organic bodies). Thus his view of sociology is that
it must study the processes of organization (the physiology) into structures (the morphology). There is a parallel, Spencer argued, between
the general mode of analysis of the structures and functions of in-

14. Ibid., p. 45.
15. Ibid.
16. Ibid.
17. Herbert Spencer, *Principles of Biology* (New York: Appleton, 1864-1867).

dividual organisms and "social organisms" composed of such individuals. Of course, social structures are "far more modifiable, far more dependent on conditions that are variable"[18] than are the structure and processes of individual organisms. Thus

> to make the parallel, and further explain the nature of the Social Sciences, we must say that the morphology and physiology of Society, instead of corresponding to the morphology of physiology of Man, correspond rather to morphology and physiology in general.[19]

Moreover, much like the Linnean classification system for individual organisms into orders, classes, families, suborders, and the like, we must be attuned to the fact that patterns of social organization may similarly be classified into varying types on the basis of their morphological and physiological characteristics. Cutting across all such types are certain common structures and processes; yet for each type, there are also distinctive characteristics unique to that type. For

> just as Biology discovers certain general traits of development, structure, and function, holding through all organisms, others holding throughout certain great groups, others throughout certain subgroups these contain; so Sociology has to recognize truths of social development, structure, and function, that some of them are universal, some of them general, some of them special.[20]

The goal of sociology should initially be to understand the basic processes underlying the elaboration of structure. Drawing from his work on biology and anticipating his principles of sociology soon to be published, he argued (1) that aggregation of individuals requires some organization and (2) that social organization involves differentiation and coordination. Thus the most fundamental topics of sociological inquiry are as follows: aggregation of units, their structural differentiation, and their modes of integration. Furthermore, there is a pattern to these processes. As aggregates grow, they differentiate; as growth encourages further differentiation, regulatory (political) structures differentiate from operative (socioeconomic) structures in order to coordinate the activities of operative structures. Subsequent differentiation occurs in both the regulatory and operative structures, and eventually

18. *The Study of Sociology,* p. 58.
19. Ibid., p. 59.
20. Ibid.

separate distributive structures (communication, transportation) differentiate.[21]

These points of emphasis anticipate by twenty years Durkheim's emphasis on such "morphological" features as size, number of parts, arrangement, and the nature of relations among parts in *The Division of Labor*.[22] Indeed, his comparison of mechanical and organic solidarity in The Division of Labor is made in terms of these variables,[23] and his discussion of evolution in both *The Division of Labor* and *Rules* is essentially the same as Spencer's (as will become evident in later chapters). The critical point is that over one hundred years ago, Spencer had a clear vision of the thrust of a structural sociology that is, I feel, still very relevant: relations among population size, its patterns of differentiation, and its modes of social integration.

METHODOLOGICAL DILEMMAS OF SOCIOLOGY

Having established in the opening three chapters of *The Study of Sociology* that there are laws of social organization to be discovered and that these laws revolve around the forms of social aggregation, differentiation, and integration, Spencer devoted the remainder of his rules on the sociological method to the problems inherent in sociological inquiry. For he recognized that from "the intrinsic natures of its facts, from our own natures as observers of the facts to be observed, there arise impediments in the way of Sociology greater than those in the way of any other science."[24]

With respect to "the intrinsic nature of the facts to be observed," Spencer recognized that precise measurement of social phenomena is more difficult in sociology than in other sciences. Many of the phenomena of sociology are "not of a directly-perceptible-kind" and cannot be measured by instruments in the same way as the subject matter of astronomy, chemistry, and physics.[25] This problem leads us in two potential directions: We either give up trying to be a science, or

21. Ibid., pp. 60-63.

22. Émile Durkheim, *The Division of Labor in Society* (New York: Free Press, 1947, originally published in 1893); see Steven Luke's *Émile Durkheim: His Life and Work* (London: Allen Lane, 1973), pp. 86-95 for further discussion on this point.

23. See Leonard Beeghley's and my *The Emergence of Sociological Theory* (Homewood, Illinois: Dorsey Press, 1981), p. 339.

24. *The Study of Sociology*, p. 72.

25. Ibid.

we seek to develop ways to measure events in the social universe. Spencer clearly advocated the latter, whereas many contemporary sociologists have simply allowed the former to immobilize inquiry.

In regard to "our own natures" as a source of bias in observing the facts, Spencer acknowledged this to be a major obstacle. On the more cognitive side, sociologists take with them modes of thinking, reasoning, and intellectual strategy that have served them in the past, whereas on the emotional side, humans always have feelings, beliefs, and other reactions to the events they study. Thus it is difficult to approach social events without a set of biases, stemming either from intellectual style or from emotionally laden reactions to social phenomena.

Related to these biases is the simple fact that observers of social facts occupy a social position in relation to the phenomena under investigation. For in no other science has "the inquirer to investigate the properties of an aggregate in which he is himself included."[26] Thus depending on one's position in the social facts to be observed, biases inevitably follow.

Having outlined in general terms these methodological problems, Spencer then launched into a more detailed analysis of each. After this analysis, he then proposed a strategy for mitigating them. In the following sections, I will reorganize Spencer's discussion in order to highlight the prominent points.

Problems in Selecting Research Problems

For Spencer, a science of sociology should be concerned with conducting research on the more generic and basic processes underlying aggregation, differentiation, and integration. Observations should be on the more general properties of the social universe, not on the time-bound, particular, and historically specific. Only to the extent that observation of such properties is used to shed light on the more generic can it be useful to science. There are, however, some fundamental impediments to making these kinds of observations.

One of these impediments is the fact that sociological research problems can be swayed by "public moods and passions."[27] As the general public becomes interested in, or even passionate about, some event or process, sociologists are likely to do research on this event. What

26. Ibid., p. 74.
27. Ibid., p. 75.

the general public sees as important is not necessarily what is sociologically important; yet there is always a temptation to do research on "marketable" events.

Another major impediment to objective research is the narrow, self-seeking interests of those who collect data and those who want it collected. The ideals of science are often supplemented by the narrow career and professional interests of researchers to make money or a reputation or to achieve some other goal that is unrelated to observations on generic properties of social systems. Similarly, organizations finance and collect data in order to "benefit those who reap incomes from them,"[28] and so organizationally funded research always biases data collection toward self-seeking concerns and away from general scientific concerns.

Yet another impediment to research is the tendency to collect data on sensational or highly visible phenomena.[29] Such visible phenomena may not be enduring or generic to human organization, and thus observations on them are not likely to increase knowledge and understanding of human organization. If the events are transitory, then we have simply observed a passing event, whereas if they are only a surface manifestation of a more basic process, we are not likely to have penetrated the surface and looked at the more sociologically significant underlying process.[30]

Still another source of bias in sociological research stems from the very act of accumulating data. As particular observational techniques are used and as certain types of data are collected, the way in which phenomena are examined can become skewed.[31] Alternative techniques and data sets are discouraged by the very dominance of the previous techniques. Moreover, individuals come to have vested interests in collecting data in certain ways, and as a result, they discourage alternatives. The very act of data accumulation can circumscribe our sociological imaginations and the research problems that we select for study.

Finally, there are a host of intellectual, personal, emotional, and positional biases built into the research process.[32] Because investigators

28. Ibid., p. 83.
29. Ibid., p. 92.
30. Ibid., p. 96.
31. Ibid., pp. 90-92.
32. Spencer devotes several chapters to these topics (see *The Study of Sociology*, pp. 113-292).

are more than neutral outsiders to social phenomena, they have preconceptions about them. Some of these preconceptions are intellectual in that investigators become so committed to a certain viewpoint—or "paradigm" in modern jargon—that they define away certain research problems as relevant or important. Other preconceptions are emotional and usually involve evaluating the social world in terms of an ideology that limits what is seen as a "relevant" topic of research. And still other preconceptions come from one's location in social structures. For example, a high-ranking person or one in academia is likely to define research problems very differently than a low-ranking individual or one outside academia.

Thus there are numerous obstacles to selecting research problems that focus on generic social structures and processes. In turn, these problems are compounded by related problems in collecting accurate data on the social world, regardless of the guiding research problem.

Gathering Accurate Data

The problems of personal bias—intellectual, emotional, and positional—immediately present themselves when making observations and collecting data on social events.[33] Intellectually, scholars rarely wish to see their "cherished hypothesis" disproved, and so they can deliberately or inadvertently skew data collection to sustain their views. Emotionally, scholars rarely will collect or accept observations that go against their ideological commitments. Positionally, the wealthy, the powerful, and the privileged in and outside of academia will infrequently collect data that call into question their situation, whereas the poor, the disenfranchised, and the marginal will not collect or accept data that reflect badly on them. Thus personal biases of humans who have intellectual and emotional commitments, and have places to hold in the structure of society, operate to distort the data collection process.

Aside from these problems of "humans studying humans," there is the related problem of understanding the "meaning" of a situation to those involved. Sociology is the study of meaningful action and organization, and so it is important to know how actors think, calculate, evaluate, and emote.[34] But we are all "outsiders" to each other's

---

33. Ibid.
34. As Spencer, ibid., p. 114, noted, "in dealing with other beings and interpreting their actions, we must represent their thoughts and feelings in terms of our own. The

mental processes, and so there is always a problem of putting ourselves as researchers in the place of those we study.

Another obstacle to data collection stems from the fact that research is always conducted at a point in time. But social processes flow over time; hence, our data catch only a cross section of what is almost always a longer term process.[35] And even if we collect data at varying points in time, we cannot be sure that we have collected data at the critical or representative points in a social process. We can, therefore, never be certain that we have not missed the essential and basic elements of social phenomena.

Finally, the social world exists and operates at different levels and varying configurations of elements. As we collect more data, we penetrate new levels and uncover additional configurations. As we do so, the causal connections become more complex and difficult to understand. Thus the more we probe, the less we know and the less we know what to do next. This is particularly likely in science such as sociology. For in sociology, we must study phenomena in natural settings that typically reveal many confounding factors and that, as a consequence, make it hard to sort them out from more basic and generic dynamics.

RESOLVING RESEARCH DILEMMAS

Unlike many who were later to catalogue this list of obstacles to conducting sociological research, Spencer did not abandon a commitment to maintaining a *science* of sociology. Methodological problems exist in all sciences, and although those in sociology are —Spencer felt—greater than in the other sciences, they can and must be overcome.

Spencer's proposal for how these methodological problems can be overcome cannot appease those who simply wish to abandon scientific sociology. Yet, his advice is worth considering. The underlying argument is that sociologists must develop the "right mental discipline."[36] They must be constantly aware of these problems and sources of bias, and they must be willing to look at their own work

---

difficulty is that in so representing them, we can never be more than partially right, and are frequently very wrong."

35. Ibid., p. 102-115.
36. Ibid., pp. 314-315.

and that of others with a critical eye that such disciplined awareness can encourage.

Such discipline can be achieved by studying the other sciences and by recognizing that there is a natural, though always antagonistic, division of labor between abstract and concrete thought or between theory and research:

> We meet with a kindred antagonism among the actions of the intellect itself, between perceiving and reasoning. Men who have aptitudes for accumulating observations are rarely men given to generalizing; while men given to generalizing are men who, mostly (use) the facts of others.[37]

There is very sound advice in his words, for in its quest for "theories of the middle range,"[38] contemporary sociology has tried to make researchers out of theorists and theorists out of researchers.[39] For research that does not at least pretend "to test theory" (however contrived the effort) is discouraged, whereas theory without a corresponding data set is "grand theory" or "too speculative." Such politically imposed "discipline" by the editors of journals is not what Spencer would have advocated. Rather, there are differences between the mental processes involved in producing abstract theory and those in collecting data; and to deny this difference—as much of American sociology does—is to subvert the process of scientific discovery.

The alternative, Spencer argued, is to look closely at other sciences and see how they approach problems. For in appreciating the differences[40] among "abstract sciences" such as logic and mathematics, the "abstract-concrete" such as physics and chemistry, and the "concrete" such as geology, we can recognize the diversity of mental processes in science and we can, as a result, develop the "right discipline" for mitigating the inherent obstacles to sociological inquiry.

Lack of familiarity with the abstract sciences "leaves the mind without due sense of *necessity of relation*"[41] and so, without some training in mathematics (as opposed to statistics, I should add) and in logic, we will lack the "discipline of mind" necessary for develop-

37. Ibid., p. 315.

38. Robert K. Merton, *Social Theory and Social Structure* (New York: Free Press, 1968).

39. See my various critiques of this failure to create a division of theoretical and research labor.

40. *The Study of Sociology,* p. 318.

41. Ibid., p. 316 (italics in original).

ing abstract statements about fundamental relations in the social universe.

Training in the abstract-concrete sciences, Spencer argued, encourages a concern with cause and effect. For

> by cultivation of the Abstract-Concrete Sciences, there is produced a further habit of thought, not otherwise produced, which is essential to right thinking in general; and, by implication, to right thinking in Sociology. Familiarity with the various orders of physical and chemical phenomena, gives distinctiveness and strength to the consciousness of *cause and effect* (italics in original).[42]

Yet, Spencer warned that exclusive concern with cause and effect generates two tendencies—"the tendency to contemplate singularly those factors which it is the aim to disentangle and identify and measure; and the tendency to rest (on) the results"[43] without examining the larger, complex of relations within which such proximate causes operate.[44] There is, I suspect, some sound advice here for a discipline that has, over the last two decades, become intellectually myopic with excessive causal modeling.

Finally, training in the concrete sciences gives us a sensitivity to the "products" that result from the operation of causal and relational forces. That is, the abstract sciences give us a sense for the forms of relations among phenomena, and the abstract-concrete sciences give us a view of causal connections of phenomena. But without a corresponding concern with the products—in sociology's case, types of social structures—that emerge from basic processes, our knowledge of the social world will be incomplete.[45]

Thus by training in other sciences, it is possible to perform sociological analysis that mitigates against the problems and obstacles of sociological inquiry. In a sense, Spencer argued that adequate sociological training involves training at each level of Comte's famous "hierarchy of the sciences."[46] But unlike Comte, whose contribution is recognized for having seen "the connection between the Science of Life and the Science of Society," Spencer proposed a particular set

42. Ibid., p. 318.
43. Ibid., p. 320.
44. Ibid., p. 321.
45. Ibid., p. 325.
46. Comte, *Positive Philosophy*.

of guidelines for studying sociology. Two of these anticipate his functionalism:

(1) Recognize that structures do operate in a larger social context and do contribute to the overall functioning of the social whole.[47]
(2) Recognize that "while . . . each society, and each successive phase of each society, presents conditions more or less special . . . there are certain general conditions which, in every society, must be fulfilled to a considerable extent before it can hold together."[48]

And a third guideline stresses his emphasis on macrostructural dynamics:

(3) Recognize that the dynamics of social organization reside in the processes of aggregation, growth, differentiation, and integration.[49]

Such were Spencer's earlier rules of the sociological method; and although he chose unfortunately to introduce some of his moralistic preachings near the end of this book, the bulk of his analysis is still relevant. We would no doubt want to throw out the functionalism, but his analysis of the problems of sociology, of the proper ways to think about social processes, and of the basic structural properties of the social world are still good advice. And for their time (1872-1873) they are remarkably insightful.

It continually amazes me that at a time when we fall all over ourselves teasing every nuance from Marx's dialectical and historical method, when we worship the few pages by Weber on method, and when we trace our ancestry to the Durkheimian structural approach, the most sophisticated of the methodological treatises of early sociology goes unnoticed. But this tragedy—the product of sociology's intellectual bigotry—is compounded by most sociologists' ignorance of Spencer's substantive work, to which I now turn.

47. *The Study of Sociology*, p. 330.
48. Ibid., p. 374.
49. Ibid., p. 347.

3

The First General Systems Theorist

THE RISE AND FALL OF GENERAL SYSTEMS THEORY

In 1954, the Society for General Systems Research organized in order to

> (1) investigate the isomorphy of concepts, laws, and models in various fields, and to help in useful transfers from one field to another; (2) encourage the development of adequate theoretical models in fields which lack them; (3) minimize the duplication of theoretical effort in different fields; (4) promote the unity of science through improving communication among specialists.[1]

For two decades, the goals of "general systems theory" captured the imagination of social scientists. Because the physical, biological, and social universes seem to reveal systemic properties, perhaps it would be possible to employ common concepts and propositions to undertand all systems—physical, biological, and social. Most general systems theorists began with basic concepts from physics—matter, energy, entropy—and then added concepts from the "new information sciences," such as cybernetics.[2]

1. As quoted in Ludwig von Bertalanffy, *General Systems Theory* (New York: Braziller, 1968), p. 15. Actually, the idea of developing a general systems approach started decades earlier.
2. See my *The Structure of Sociological Theory*. 3rd edition (Homewood, Illinois: Dorsey Press, 1982), pp. 450-453 for a review of these concepts.

In all of this burst of intellectual activity, there was an almost euphoric optimism about the prospects for generating common models for different types of systemic dimension of the universe and for unifying, at the most abstract level, the various sciences. In the end, general systems theory came crashing down and now exists in relative intellectual obscurity. The reasons for this meteoric rise and fall, as George Ritzer has phrased it,[3] are diverse, but they revolve around the fact that although all systems of the universe may indeed evidence common properties, it is the unique properties and processes of systems that are more interesting to investigators. What cuts across physical, biological, and sociocultural systems is far less interesting than what makes each unique. Moreover, the concepts used to portray common properties and processes of systems must, by necessity, be so general as to seem empty and obvious to those working out the details of one systemic context. For example, to portray cultural values, norms, beliefs, and technologies as "information" is interesting, and perhaps it allows us to see parallels with informational codes on the chromosomes of organisms; but does it really allow us to do anything new intellectually? Does viewing values as information change the way we look at values and analyze them? Or, is the concept of information simply old wine in new, opaque bottles?

Increasingly, as the promise of general systems theory failed to inspire social scientists, two kinds of activity ensued among its practitioners. One line of activity involved the highly technical development of mathematical models on a very narrow range of topics; and the other tact led to the development of grand conceptual schemes for integrating diverse sciences. The former has typically been too technical and too esoteric to be of interest to practicing sociologists, whereas the latter has not been well received in sociology where we were just beginning to dismantle the grand Parsonian analytical scheme.[4]

I have touched briefly on the history of general systems theory because I want to stress the fact that this "new" effort was, in fact, very old. Herbert Spencer had made a very similar effort to view the systems of the universe in terms of certain basic principles. Indeed, his Synthetic Philosophy, as he called it, was a general systems approach to social reality. And, had those who were interested in constructing grand, synthetic schemes been aware of Spencer, they could

---

3. George Ritzer, *Sociological Theory* (New York: Knopf, 1983), p. 450.
4. For example, see James Grier Miller, *Living Systems* (New York: McGraw-Hill, 1978).

have saved themselves a great deal of wasted intellectual effort. For both the promise and failings of a general systems approach can be found in Spencer's early works.[5] In Appendix A, I have listed the program of Spencer's Synthetic Philosophy as he saw it in 1860, which was followed in 1862 with the publication of the initial work in his general systems approach.[6] In Appendix B, I have listed the basic "laws" that James G. Miller[7] inducted over a twenty-year period in building a general systems approach to "living systems" that operate at seven levels: cells, organs, organisms, groups, organizations, societies, and systems of societies. These laws in Appendix B should be compared with those developed by Spencer in *First Principles* and *Principles of Sociology* (see Chapter 5), both of which appeared one hundred years earlier. The principles are virtually the same, and yet Miller, his supporters, and his detractors seem unaware of this fact.

It is perhaps a bit extreme to argue that the end result of a general systems approach was the rediscovery of Spencer's Synthetic Philosophy. Indeed, scholars such as Walter Buckley[8] would consider Spencer's functionalism the antithesis of his views on the proper general systems approach. Yet if one actually looks at the product of his and others' efforts, there is not a dramatic difference between modern efforts and those developed by Spencer. I will not fully document this assertion in this chapter alone. But as I outline in this chapter Spencer's general laws, or "first principles," of the universe, and as I present in subsequent chapters how he used them to analyze sociocultural systems, I think that this assertion will be supported. Let us, therefore, see what the first general systems theorist in sociology had to say.

SPENCER'S "FIRST PRINCIPLES"

The Fundamental Processes: Evolution and Dissolution

In 1862, Spencer published *First Principles*[9] in which he delineated the "cardinal" or "first" principles of the universe. Like any general

---

5. In particular, Herbert Spencer, *First Principles* (New York: A. L. Burt, 1880 edition of a work originally published in 1862).

6. Ibid., pp. II-XI

7. Miller, *Living Systems,* see also Turner, op. cit., p. 461.

8. Walter Buckley, *Sociology and Modern Systems Theory* (Englewood Cliffs, NJ: Prentice-Hall, 1967).

9. Spencer, *First Principles.*

systems theorist, Spencer sought to articulate those highly abstract laws that, he felt, governed the relations among inorganic, organic, psychological, and superorganic (societal) relations. That is, relations among physical, organic, psychological, and social units operate in terms of certain underlying processes that can be articulated as abstract laws of the entire universe.[10] Celestial bodies, chemical compounds, cells, organic evolution, cognitions, and social aggregations all reveal common underlying processes; and although each level of reality in the universe evidences distinctive processes, they also reveal certain basic dynamics.

These processes are to be conceptualized as "evolution" and "dissolution," or in more modern terms, structuring and destructuring of elements.[11] The matter of the universe is always in a process of (1) aggregating to form more complex structures, (2) fluctuating between phases of structuring and destructuring alternate, (3) disintegrating as elements begin to destructure. Indeed, Spencer borrowed from the physics of his time, and like systems theorists today, the elements of the universe are governed by the laws of entropy (and negentropy). The universe is, therefore, a constant state of tension as elements aggregate and become structured, as they stand for a time in equilibrium, and as they dissolve or disaggregate and destructure. As he noted,[12]

> there is always a differential progress toward either integration or disintegration. During the earlier part of the cycle of changes, the integration predominates—there goes on what we call growth. The middle part of the cycle is usually characterized, not by equilibrium between the integrating and disintegrating processes, but by alternative excesses of them. And the cycle closes with a period in which the disintegration, beginning to predominate, eventually puts a stop to integration, and undoes what integration had originally done.

I emphasize this view of the universe because Spencer's work has incorrectly been interpreted as purely evolutionary. He is too often seen as postulating a lineal evolutionary view of the universe, but in fairness, his analysis of evolutionary processes must be placed in the

10. As can be seen from Appendix A, Spencer also felt that these principles guided "morality." His scheme was, therefore, for more philosophical than contemporary general systems theory.

11. *First Principles,* pp. 241-249.

12. Ibid., p. 246.

context of his analysis of dissolution. Spencer was not a naive child of The Enlightenment who saw the social world as progressing to a desired end-state. Marx and Durkheim were much more the children of this naive view than Spencer. Although Spencer had a moralistic vision of the "good society"—as did Marx and Durkheim—his underlying view of the universe is cyclical—evolution, fluctuation in precarious equilibrium, and then dissolution. His work should be viewed as anticipating Pareto's [13] mode of the analysis rather than the optimistic evolutionism of Marx, Durkheim, and others in the late nineteenth century.

Spencer's "law of evolution" is often quoted out of this broader context as[14]

> an integration of matter and concomitant dissipation of motion; during which the matter passes from an indefinite incoherent homogeneity to a definite coherent heterogeneity; and during which the retained motion undergoes a parallel transformation.

True, this is his definition of evolution, but it is only one side of the equation. The other side is dissolution. For as he carefully pointed out, evolution and dissolution are on opposite sides of the same coin. Evolution eventually sets into motion forces of dissolution. Spencer saw that there is always an "antagonism" between evolution and dissolution as one gains a "temporary triumph" over the other. And thus

> evolution under its simplest and most general aspect is the integration of matter and concomitant dissipation of motion; while dissolution is the absorption of motion and concomitant disintegration of matter.[15]

For Spencer, then, the goal of his Synthetic Philosophy, or his general systems theory, is to conceptualize the processes of evolution *and* dissolution in terms of one set of abstract principles. I have started in the middle of his *First Principles* to emphasize this fact. But I have not explained what initially seem like awkward terms— "homogeneity," and "heterogeneity"; "matter," "motion"; and the like—because I wanted to emphasize that these concepts and

13. Vilfred Pareto, *Treatise on General Sociology* (1907), translated and published with the unfortunate title of "The Mind and Society" (New York: Harcourt Brace Jovanovich, 1935).

14. *First Principles,* p. 343.

15. Ibid., p. 247.

the laws into which they are incorporated are intended to explain, at the most abstract level, both evolution *and* dissolution. Now, let me return to the laws themselves that appear before the discussion of evolution and dissolution.

The Laws of the Universe

Spencer drew his basic principles from the physics of his time. The principles, themselves, are less crucial than the effort to articulate the underlying "truths which unify concrete phenomena belonging to all divisions of nature."[16]

Principle 1 asserts "the indestructibility of matter" which is, of course, not really true by today's physics.[17] Moreover, it is less crucial to his scheme than Principles 2 and 3, which proclaim, respectively, the "continuity of motion" and the "persistence of force." By these Spencer meant that matter moving in a given direction will continue to do so and that the force behind it (that is, what causes the motion) will persist in a given direction unless it confronts a resisting force or collides with other matter or until "friction" dissipates the motion. From these three principles, Spencer generated what he termed three "deductions." One deduction is that force is "transformable"; another is that motion follows the line of least resistance; and the third is that motion is rhythmic (gyrations, oscillations, epochs, cycles, etc.).

Much of the strange vocabulary of Spencer's definitions for evolution and dissolution can now be better understood. However inadequately, he sought to see if all realms of nature could be interpreted in light of several universal, or "first," principles. It is the *combined* operation of these principles that explains the dynamics of various systems in the universe:[18]

> Having seen that matter is indestructable, motion continuous, and force persistent—having seen that forces are everywhere undergoing transformation, and that motion, always following the line of least resistance, is invariable rhythmic, it remains to discover the similarly invariable formula expressing the combined consequences of the actions thus separately formulated.

16. Ibid., p. 236.
17. Ibid.
18. Ibid., p. 239.

This discovery of the "combined consequences" will revolve around an analysis of "continuous redistribution of matter and motion."[19] And it is at this point that Spencer introduced the reader in *First Principles* to evolution and dissolution as the basic processes that express the combined consequences of his first principles.

Principles of Evolution[20]

In trying to explain evolution, or the building of structure, Spencer sought initially to develop several additional principles. These principles are directed at the problem of why evolution involves an increasing complexity—increases in the number of different units and their integration—of structure.

One principle is the inherent "instability of the homogeneous."[21] The basic idea is that undifferentiated units are not integrated by ties of mutual interdependence. As a consequence, when "matter in motion" from external forces hits a homogeneous mass, its elements are more readily scattered because there are not strong connective ties of mutual interdependence. As their "retained motion" disperses them to varying environments, they are more likely to become different because they each confront unique forces in their new environments. Conversely, heterogeneous masses, where units are interconnected by webs of mutual dependence, resist disruption by external forces and, hence, can maintain their structure more effectively than homogeneous masses where elements are mere segments or duplications of each other. Thus homogeneous masses are subject to disruption, dispersion, and subsequent differentiation; and as forces consistently act in this way on homogeneous masses, complexity, is built up in the universe. Spencer felt that this principle helps account for a wide variety of evolutionary processes—for the building of solar systems, the creation of chemical compounds, the emergence of new species, the elaboration of cognitive complexity, and the growing complexity of societal social systems.

Another related principle is "the multiplication of effects."[22] As a force disperses the elements of a homogeneous mass in different directions, the retained motion takes the elements to new environments and often to "collisions" with other masses. Thus, over time, as once

19. Ibid., p. 240.
20. Ibid., pp. 241-418.
21. Ibid., p. 347.
22. Ibid., p. 373.

homogeneous elements adjust to new environments and to the motion of other objects, their differences multiply. For as long as there is retained motion, they move into new environments; and as they encounter new elements with their own retained motion, some of this force behind the motion is "transferred" sending them in new directions. And so over time, increased complexity is built into the universe. For example, as a once homogeneous population flees oppressive conditions (the force behind their motion) and seeks to survive in different social niches and in different types of societies, their differences multiply. Their values, beliefs, social behaviors, and perhaps even biological features (skin color) are altered by adjustments to new environments and by transference of motion (say, new political conditions or intermarriage) to and from others in these new environments.

A third principle on "the effects of segregation"[23] explains how multiplication of differences occurs. New environments always present masses with their own motion as propelled by varying forces. Each environment presents a somewhat different collage of such forces; and thus, as any object or mass moves to a new environment, the motion of these other objects is transferred, thereby altering the force and motion of the mass. Conversely, the object entering an environment transfers its motion—especially if the force behind this motion is great—to the existing masses in the environment, thereby changing both the mass and its new environment. Such processes assure that environments separated in time and space will be different and segregated from each other. For example, conquering armies may be similar as they leave their home base, but as they enter different regions, the segregation of these regions in terms of culture, politics, economics, and other forces assures that the effects of the armies as they march into a region will vary; conversely, the unique configuration of forces and motions in the region will "transfer" to the armies, thereby making them somewhat different. Thus segregation increases the multiplication of effects; and at the same time, it operates to maintain differences in environments.

Thus the course of evolution is to increase differences, and hence, complexity in the universe. Of course, at some point the retained motion can begin to decrease as it encounters resistance. And so, the structure that has been built up can begin to fluctuate and then to dissolve. Evolution must always be viewed as occurring within the constraints

23. Ibid., p. 397.

imposed by the forces of entropy. For as the forces behind the retained motion of objects dissipates, then the likelihood of dissolution increases, unless new forces enter the system. When such forces do not
exist, or simply overwhelm the system and are not transferred to its
elements (thereby giving them new motion), then the system dissolves
and the complexity that has been built up decreases.

There is, then, an inherent tendency toward dissolution built into
the very process of evolution. As will be recalled, evolution involves
"a change from a less coherent form to a more coherent form, consequent on the dissipation of motion and integration of matter."[24] Thus
the very process in integration creates a decrease in the vital forces
behind motion that aggregated masses and that allow for the multiplication of effects in segregated environments to operate. For example,
as the masses that constitute a solar system become integrated, they
also begin the long process of decay. Or as diverse populations of people become organized politically, much of the vitality and force that
prompted such organization in the first place can be lost, initiating
a more stagnant system that can, over time, dissolve.

Thus evolution invokes the aggregation of matter, deflections and
transference of motion to create complexity, and then the dissipation
of the force that created such complexity through integration of matter. Much of the strange vocabulary in Spencer's definition of evolution must be understood in light of his general systems approach. For
he was addressing not only sociocultural evolution, but evolution in
the entire universe. We can now better appreciate the definition cited
earlier: "evolution is an integration of matter and concomitant dissipation of motion; during which the matter passes from an indefinite in-
coherent homogeneity to a definite coherent heterogeneity; and during which the retained motion undergoes a parallel transformation."[25]
And yet, Spencer asked:[26]

> Can things increase in heterogeneity through all future time? Or must
> there be a degree which the differentiation and integration of matter
> and motion cannot pass? . . . Whether we watch concrete processes,
> or whether we consider the question in the abstract, we are alike taught
> that evolution has an impossible limit.

24. Ibid., p. 283.
25. Ibid., p. 343.
26. Ibid., p. 418.

> The redistributions of matter that go on around us are ever being brought
> to conclusions by the dissipation of the motions that which effect
> them.

And thus, built into the process of evolution are inevitable equilibrating
processes and, eventually, dissolution.

Principles of Equilibration[27]

Immediately after his analysis of evolution in the universe, Spencer
examined equilibrium. Evolution, or the aggregation, differentiation,
and integration of elements, inevitably leads to a state of equilibrium.
For in all systems of the universe, there is

> a process toward equilibration. That universal co-existence of antagonistic
> forces which, as we before saw, necessitates the universality of rhythm,
> and which, as we before saw, necessitates decomposition of every force
> into divergent forces, at the same time necessitates the ultimate establish-
> ment of a balance. Every motion being a motion under resistance is
> continually suffering deductions, and these unceasing deductions finally
> result in the cessation of the motion.[28]

Spencer thus borrowed his conception of equilibrium from his interpretation of physics. He visualized equilibrating processes in the social,
organic, and psychological realms as a special case of these more
fundamental equilibrating processes of the physical universe. Indeed,
most of his discussion consists of examples from astrophysics, chemistry,
biology, psychology, and only briefly, sociology. In so doing, he
conceptualized four orders of equilibrium.[29] First, there are projectiles
that, as they move through an environment, will encounter resistance
and quickly cease their motion. Second, there are processes in which
the motion of elements can stand in equilibrium only temporarily
because its motion must overcome counterforces surrounding it (a
spinning top temporarily overcoming the effects of wind, surface
friction, and most important, gravity being good examples). Third,
and most critical to sociology, is an equilibrium that is "dependent"
upon the infusion from the outside of energy that can overcome
the counterforces in the environment (for example, an engine dependent upon fuel, and organism dependent upon food, and a social
system dependent upon well fed and motivated actors being con-

27. Ibid., p. 418.
28. Ibid., p. 414.
29. Ibid., p. 421-422.

spicuous examples). And fourth, in contrast to such a "dependent equilibrium" is a state of "independent equilibrium" where elements encounter so little resistance and dissipation of motion and where there are so few counterforces in the environment that the equilibrium lasts for very long periods of time (the solar system being an example).

Thus, depending upon the type of equilibrium involved, elements can sustain their equilibrium for varying periods of time. Sociocultural equilibrium depends upon a constant infusion of energy from the environment to sustain a given structure in that environment. Moreover, for evolution to occur, the elements must increase the flow of energy from the environment to support and integrate a larger aggregation of differentiated elements. Thus heterogeneity can only advance to the point where the intake of energy from the environment is equal "as many specializations and combination of parts as there are specialized and combined forces to be met."[30]

Not only can the system of elements—say, an entire society or solar system—be seen as in equilibrium with an external environment, but each of the elements themselves—the persons or groups in society and the planets in a solar system—stands in equilibrium (or in an evolutionary or structuring phase) to its environment—that is, the other elements as well as the environment of the total system. There are several important implications to this fact. One is that those elements that have little force behind their motion or that encounter the greatest resistance will reach equilibrium faster than those with great force or little resistance. Another implication is that as these "weaker forces" lose their motion, only the stronger ones remain, and as a consequence, a system of elements may wobble or oscillate dramatically until these remaining "strong forces" dissipate. Thus, for example, a society that is no longer growing and is close to equilibrium if not dissolution in its environment may experience considerable turmoil— revolutions, counterrevolutions, and the like—because only the strong forces (say, politically powerful segments, highly motivated actors, and the like) have not reached an equilbruim point.

Thus Spencer's conceptualization of equilibrium forces the recognition that the evolution or structuring of a system occurs relative to the forces that dissipate the motion of elements as they aggregate, differentiate, and integrate. For sociocultural systems, this structuring is dependent upon the capacity of energy (food, materials, and motives)

30. Ibid., p. 424.

to exceed the resistance of environmental forces and social "friction." When this intake of energy exceeds these forces, evolution exists. When it is only equal to them, then equilibrium occurs. And when it is less than these forces, then dissolution ensues.

It is at this point that Spencer prepared to move on to a discussion of dissolution, the last substantive chapter in *First Principles*. But ever the philosopher, he closes by asking:[31]

> If evolution of every kind is an increase in complexity of structure and function that is incidental to the universal process of equilibrium, and if equilibrium must end in complete rest, what is the fate toward which all things tend? If the solar system is slowly dissipating its forces—if the sun is losing its heat at a rate which will tell in millions of years—if with diminution of the sun's radiations there must go on a diminution in the activity of geologic and meteorologic processes as well as in the quantity of vegetal and animal existence—if man and society are similarly dependent on this supply of force that is gradually coming to an end, are we not manifestly progressing toward omnipresent death?

Principles of Dissolution

Near the end of *First Principles,* Spencer did not "dwell long on dissolution, which has none of those various and interesting aspects which evolution presents."[32] And his discussion of societal dissolution is particularly brief, which is not surprising given that he had not begun any sociological works in the early 1860s (indeed, he had yet to publish his large treatise on biology and psychology). Yet, he does enumerate several principles.

First, dissolution is the converse of evolution that involves aggregation, differentiation, and integration by virtue of increased coordination of motion. And hence, dissolution occurs when integration breaks down and the movement of parts is no longer controlled by the systemic whole. Under this condition, disaggregation and dedifferentiation occurs.

Second, as dissolution begins, the forces of the environment increase the motion of the disintegrating parts, thereby accelerating the decrease in their coordination and control. As environmental force is deflected onto poorly coordinated parts, they move off into different directions and the system collapses.

31. Ibid., p. 445.
32. Ibid., p. 449.

Third, the parts of a disintegrating system can be recombined, *if* there is a sufficiently powerful force to reaggregate them into a new system or to incorporate them into an already existing system. There is, then, the potential for evolution from the remnants of dissolution.

Fourth, the integration of parts of an equilibrated system can be sustained for long periods of time *as long as* there is no sudden change in environmental forces. If the environmental forces increase, however, then the movement of parts will increase and the capacity to hold them together will decrease.

When these general ideas are applied to sociocultural evolution, it becomes clear what Spencer is trying to communicate. As societies grow in size, they differentiate, and then integrate their new complexity through mutual interdependence *and* political authority.[33] As long as new resources are generated through conquest, technological innovation, immigration, and other processes, a social system can continue to grow and differentiate. But at some point, the resistance provided by trying to coordinate increased numbers of individuals in terms of a particular level or resources creates equilibrium. As long as the environment does not change, the society can sustain itself for long periods of time. But if new societies enter a territory, if resource levels decrease, if a national disaster occurs, or if any of many forces in the environment increase, then dissolution is initiated. Spencer argued that such has been the history of human societies as, first, equilibrated hunting and gathering societies were overcome, and then, as horticulture and agriculture societies were dissolved by the colonialism and exploitation by industrial societies.

As environmental forces (conquest by other societies, decreases in food and energy, natural disasters, etc.) weaken ties of mutual dependence and political authority, dissolution accelerates, especially if environmental forces are strong. Dissolution can be checked, however, if another society has the resources to dominate and control one that is dissolving and to create a new pattern of structure. Or, if members immigrate to new societies capable of further evolution, then their addition to these societies accelerates the growth, differentiation, and expanded integration of these host societies (it also hastens the dissolution of the society from which the immigration occurs).

---

33. Ibid., pp. 450-451. Spencer does begin to give us some idea of what his sociological analysis will look like in these closing pages, even though it is over a decade away.

SPENCER'S GENERAL SYSTEMS THEORY

I do not want to pretend that *First Principles* is a crucial work in Spencer's sociology. It is an interesting work, because it illustrates the strengths and weaknesses of a general systems approach. Like all general systems theorists, Spencer felt that there are certain isomorphic properties among all realms of the universe. Indeed, it must have been enormously exciting to write *First Principles* and to believe that one had unlocked some of the mysteries of the entire universe. One can sense this excitement in *First Principles,* just as we can see the initial burst of enthusiasm in the general systems approach.[34] Yet, there was a major flaw in Spencer's work and in much contemporary general systems theory. Whatever isomorphisms exist among realms of the universe are likely to be so general that they do not tell us much about the specific dynamics of any one realm. In *First Principles,* Spencer cites many examples of his principles, but illustrations are not the same as systematic deductions from the "first principles" to the operative processes of some specific realm.

To Spencer's credit, he went beyond *First Principles* and tried to use them as the highest order axioms in a deductive scheme that saw him first of all outline the operative processes of the biological and psychological realms. And finally, he moved to sociology. He never abandoned his view that the "first principles" were the general axioms underlying sociological processes, but by the time he got to sociology, he had become more interested in the parallels between the organic (biological) and super-organic (social system) realms. The vocabulary of *First Principles* is still prominent, but the major thrust of his analysis is to explore actual dynamics of the super-organic realm rather than to view this realm as an illustration of his first principles of the universe.

The metaphorical importance of his first principles should not, however, be underemphasized, for the basic thrust of his sociological analysis follows from them:

(1) Examine the processes of structuring (evolution) of social systems by concentrating on (a) their growth in size, (b) their patterns of differentiation, and (c) their mechanisms of integration.
(2) Examine the forces of system structure relative to the countervailing forces in the environment, with particular emphasis on (a) the effects

34. See, for example, Walter Buckley, *Modern Systems Theory.*

of resource levels, (b) the effects of other social systems, (c) the effects of ecological (climatic, geographic, and other natural) conditions.
(3) Examine the extent to which a society has reached an equilibrium point in a given environment by (a) determining the size of population and how much its mechanism of integration exceeds (b) the resource base of its environment.
(4) Examine the fluctuations and cycles inherent in the process of evolution and equilibration by analyzing the varying basis for integrating differentiated populations.
(5) Examine the process of destructuring as modes of integration become ineffective for a given population in a particular environment.

If this is all that could be said about Spencerian sociology, I would not bother to write this book. Indeed, we could legitimately look at Spencer as we currently do: an intellectual whose time has come and gone and who did not generate any really enduring ideas. But such was not the case. When Spencer actually undertook sociological analysis, he used his general systems metaphor to produce not only original but enduring sociological principles. Just as general systems theory has had to relearn the lessons clearly evident in *First Principles,* so sociological theorizing has had to rediscover Spencer's theoretical ideas.

As I mentioned in the preface to this book, there is a terrible injustice here. At a time when we pour over Marx, Weber, and Durkheim like religious scholars in the hopes of finding yet one more interesting idea, we ignore Spencer whose works are filled with ideas, many of which we misattribute to Durkheim and some of which we have rediscovered close to a century after Spencer developed them. This oversight—as well as this slighting—of Spencer's work is more than an injustice to Spencer as a scholar. It demonstrates how uncumulative sociological theory can be. Because contemporay sociologists do not like Spencer's social ideology,[35] they ignore the substance of his work. My goal in the next chapters is to highlight the importance of Spencer's theoretical ideas, without the typical prejudices about Spencer's politics and moralizing.

---

35. Neither do I.

Appendix A

In March 1860, Spencer presented the following prospectus from which I have extracted the major headings. The eventual works deviated somewhat from this early outline, but correspond in rough form to the final product that was completed in 1898.

A System of Philosophy

First Principles
>Part I: The Unknowable
>Part II: Laws of the Knowable

The Principles of Biology
>*Volume I*

>Part I: The Data of Biology
>Part II: The Inductions of Biology
>Part III: The Evolution of Life

>*Volume II*

>Part IV: Morphological Development
>Part V: Physiological Development
>Part VI: The Laws of Multiplication

The Principles of Psychology
>*Volume I*

>Part I: The Data of Psychology
>Part II: The Inductions of Psychology
>Part III: General Synthesis
>Part IV: Special Synthesis
>PartV: Physical Synthesis

>*Volume II*

>Part VI: Special Analysis
>Part VII: General Analysis
>Part VIII: Corollaries

The Principles of Sociology
>*Volume I*

>Part I: The Data of Sociology
>Part II: The Inductions of Sociology
>Part III: Political Organization

Volume II

Part IV: Ecclesiastical Organization
Part V: Ceremonial Organization
Part VI: Industrial Organization

   Volume III

Part VII: Lingual Progress
Part VIII: Intellectual Progress
Part IX: Esthetic Progress
Part X: Moral Progress
Part XI: The Consensus

The Principles of Morality
   Volume I

Part I: The Data of Morality
Part II: The Inductions of Morality
Part III: Personal Morals

   Volume II

Part IV: Justice
Part V: Negative Beneficence
Part VI: Positive Beneficence

In the 1862 version of this prospectus, as it appeared in the preface to
First Principles, Spencer noted:

In anticipation of the obvious criticism that the scheme here sketched
out is too extensive, it may be remarked that an exhaustive treatment
of each topic is not intended, but simply the establishment of *principles,* with such illustrations as are needed to make their bearings fully
understood. It may also be pointed out that, besides minor fragments,
one large division, "The Principles of Psychology," is already in great
part executed. And a further reply is, that, impossible though it may
prove to execute the whole, yet nothing can be said against an attempt
to set forth the first principles and to carry their applications as far
as circumstances permit.

This programme I have thought well to reprint for two reasons: —the
one being that readers may, from time to time, be able to ascertain
what topics are next to be dealt with, the other being that an outline
of the scheme may remain, in case it should never be completed.

London, June 5, 1862.

Appendix B

J. G. Miller's Laws of "Living Systems"[36]

(1) The larger a *living system* is, the more likely are (pp. 108-109):

    (a) patterns of structural differentiation among components
    (b) decentralized centers of decision making
    (c) interdependence of subsystems
    (d) elaborate adjustment processes
    (e) differences in input-output sensitivity of components
    (f) elaborate and varied outputs.

(2) The greater the level of structural differentiation of components in a living system is, the greater is:

    (a) the number of echelons or ranks among subsystems (p. 92)
    (b) segregation of functions (p. 109)
    (c) the ratio of information transmitted within rather than across boundaries (pp. 93, 103)

(3) The greater the ratio of information to energy/matter processed across system boundaries as negative and positive feedback is, the more likely is a living system to survive in its environment (p. 94).

(4) The more hierarchically differentiated a living system into echelons is, the more likely is:

    (a) the presence of discordant information among differentiated subsystems (p. 109)
    (b) the utilization by *decided* subsystems (high ranking) of information from memory banks than from lower ranking echelons (pp. 99-100)

(5) The greater the number of channels for processing information in a structurally differentiated living system is, the less likely are:

    (a) errors in transmission and reception of information (p. 96)
    (b) strains and tensions among subsystems (pp. 97, 107)

---

36. In this appendix, page numbers in parentheses refer to the pages in *Living Systems* on which hypotheses are initially presented. The propositions have been rephrased and regrouped for more efficient presentation. Source: Turner, *The Structure of Sociological Theory*. 3rd edition (Homewood, Illinois: Dorsey Press, 1982), p. 461.

(6) The greater the level of stress experienced by a living system from its environment is, the greater is (pp. 106-107):

    (a) the number of components devoted to its alleviation

    (b) the less manifest previous tensions among internal system components

    (c) the deviation of processes within the system, and each of its subsystems, from previously normal states

    (d) the difficulty of returning the system and subsystem processes to previously normal states after alleviation of the strain

(7) The greater the level of segregation of subsystems in a living system is, the greater is their level of conflict and the greater is the total information and/or energy/matter mobilized in each subsystem for resolving the conflict and the less information or energy/matter available for achieving overall system goals (p. 107).

4

The First Functionalist

THE BEGINNING AND END OF
ANALYTICAL FUNCTIONALISM

In 1939, the opening passage of Talcott Parsons's *The Structure of Social Action* asks:[1] "Who now reads Spencer?" The irony behind this question is that Parsons was later to become the quiescent functionalist of his time, and in the process, to rediscover Spencerian sociology.[2] It is not clear to me if Parsons read, initially rejected, forgot, and then remembered Spencer's *Principles of Sociology*[3] or if he simply forgot and then independently rediscovered the ideas in Spencer's work. But there can be little doubt that by the end of his career Parsons' action theory began to look very much like Spencer's synthetic philosophy with its emphasis on diverse realms of the universe

1. Talcott Parsons, *The Structure of Social Action* (New York: McGraw-Hill, 1937).

2. For example, his two volumes on evolution, *Societies: Evolutionary and Comparative Perspectives* and *The System of Modern Societies* (both published by Prentice-Hall, 1966 and 1971, respectively) borrows (or recreates) Spencer's evolutionary model, with modifications from Durkheim's and Weber's work.

3. Herbert Spencer, *Principles of Sociology* (1874-1896 in serial form). This work has been re-issued in varying volume numbers. References in this chapter are to the three volume edition (the third edition) issued by Appleton, New York, in 1898. In reading this long work, it is much more critical to note the parts (numbered I through VII) than the volumes, because pagination can vary with various editions.

and with the analysis of social systems emphasizing the functions of structures for meeting system needs or requisites.[4] Moreover, Parsons returned to the evolutionary theme so evident in Spencer's work— growth, differentiation, integration, and adaptation.[5] Thus the very first sociological functionalist and the last (at least hopefully so)[6] had much in common. Indeed, Parsons's formal training in biology as an undergraduate and Spencer's self-training in biology and the publication of *Principles of Biology*[7] just before writing his sociological works no doubt encouraged both of their functional analyses.

For in the end, functional analysis is based upon an organismic view of social systems. That is, societies are like organisms in that they reveal parts that operate or *function* to maintain the viability of "the body social" in a given environment. Although this idea did not originate with Spencer, he was the first to explore it with any degree of sociological precision. Comte's earlier pronouncements[8] on functional analysis certainly predate Spencer's, but they are not precise, nor are they used to analyze systematically social structures. Indeed, the use of organic analogies by Plato and others in the more distant past is more detailed than Comte's discussion. And so, it is Spencer on whom I wish to bestow the stigma, "the first true sociological functionalist."

---

4. Before his death, I asked Professor Parsons about Spencer, and he seemed unaware of the degree to which his work paralleled Spencer's.

5. See note 2.

6. I am afraid, of course, that I'm overly optimistic here, as "neo-functionalism" has emerged in Europe; and thus we will still be burdened with functional analysis in sociology.

7. Herbert Spencer, *Principles of Biology* (New York: Appleton, 1864-1867). Spencer's analysis of biology formulated several laws that are still used today. For example, the principle that, in regularly shaped bodies, the surface area increases as the square of linear dimensions and volume as the cube of these dimensions is still used today. This principle—relating size, volume, and skeletal complexity—clearly influenced Spencer's sociology (and, I should add, Durkheim's).

8. Auguste Comte, *System of Positive Philosophy 3 Volumes,* translated and condensed by H. Martineau (London: George Bell and Sons, 1896, originally published in 1854 but written serially between 1830 and 1842). See, in particular, Volume II, pp. 275-294. Moreover, in his summary of Part II of *Principles of Sociology* (p. 591), Spencer reviews the analogues of Comte, Plato, and Hobbes. He has more sympathy for Hobbes' analysis (for unlike many of Spencer's critics' claims, he stressed the "functions of" power in social systems), but concludes that it was Comte who avoided the errors of early organicists and who "not comparing the social organism to an individual organism of any one kind, held simply that the principles of organization are common to societies and animals" (ibid., p. 591).

But I also wish to stress that unlike his imitator, Talcott Parsons, Spencer's analysis is much more structural than functional. Spencer is much less concerned with the functions of a structure for maintaining the social whole than with the *pattern of structural differentiation* in social systems. Although Spencer's work is filled with analogies to organic processes, it is not nearly as "functional" as commentators often believe.

The reason that Spencer could analogize to organismic processes and avoid many of the functional traps that would plague Parsons's later work can be found in his view that both organic and societal processes are derivative of higher order laws and axioms—that is, his "first principles" discussed in the last chapter. At the analytical level, Spencer analogized as much to the physics of his time as to the biology. He illustrated his analytical points with biological analogies, but the highest order analytic principles are borrowed from physics and are directed toward understanding how social matter, force, and motion affect the structuring (evolution), destructuring (dissolution), and equilibrium (rhythmic phases) of the social world.[9]

I am stressing these points because it is important to separate the functionalism in Spencer's analysis from the structuralism. We easily forgive Durkheim for his functionalism, but we are merciless in our condemnation of Spencerian sociology for being "so functional." In what may seem like a contradiction, I believe that Spencer's functional analysis is far more sophisticated and elaborate than Durkheim's and, at the same time, less intrusive in his actual analysis.[10] For Durkheim, his analysis is *always* directed toward the "integrative" functions (that is, his moral view of what "the good society is") of a structure, whereas for Spencer, such is not the case. The moral view is highly recessive in his explicitly sociological works and the functionalism does not seem to drive analysis in the same way that it did for Durkheim, and of course, for Parsons. And just as sociology is coming to appreciate the power of Parsons's ideas when disembodied from his functionalism and as we have already done for Durkheim, so we must do for Spencer.[11] And, in Spencer's case it is easier than for either Durkeim or Parsons.

9. And the biological and psychological (or "organic") realms.

10. Even a casual comparison of *Principals of Sociology* with Durkheim's major works will, I feel, document this assertion.

11. In several works, I have tried to do this. See Leonard Beeghley's and my book *The Emergence of Sociological Theory* (Homewood, Illinois: Dorsey Press, 1981), Chapter 5 as well as my "The Forgotten Giant: Herbert Spencer's Theoretical Models

Such is my goal in this chapter: to present Spencer's functionalism and, in so doing, to separate it from his more enduring analysis of social processes. I have little doubt that his functionalism had a great impact—too great, I am positive—on sociological theory. For despite his protests about Spencer, Durkheim borrowed his functionalism.[12] I also am sure that anthropological functionalists, such as Malinowski,[13] took from Spencer. And, I suspect that Parsons[14] subliminally borrowed from Spencer's functionalism (as well as his structuralism; see later chapters). There was, then, something very intriguing about Spencer's functionlism; my goal in this chapter is to outline just what made his functionalism so interesting.

PRINCIPLES OF SOCIOLOGY, PART I:
ON PRELIMINARY CONSIDERATIONS

Like most functionalists, such as Malinowski and Parsons,[15] Spencer began by distinguishing the inorganic, organic, and super-organic realms. Spencer emphasized all of these realms on the opening page of *Principles of Sociology;* they follow from the first principles outlined in 1862.[16] His preceding treatises on *Principles of Biology*[17] and *Principles of Psychology*[18] are concerned with organic evolution. Thus for Spencer, psychology is the biological science concerned with "phenomena distinguished as psychical, which the most evolved organic aggregates display."[19] In contrast to organic aggregates is the super-organic realm that involves the coordination among individual organisms. The super-organic includes insect societies as well as organiz-

---

and Principles," *European Review of the Social Sciences* XIX (59, 1981), pp. 79-98 and "Durkheim's and Spencer's Principles of Social Organization," *Sociological Perspectives* 27 (January, 1984), pp. 21-32.

12. Émile Durkheim's *The Division of Labor in Society* (New York: Free Press, 1947, originally published in 1893) borrows heavily from Spencer while constantly criticizing Spencerian sociology—an interesting tact, to say the least.

13. See, for example, Bronislaw Malinowski, *A Scientific Theory of Culture and Other Essays* (London: Oxford University Press, 1964).

14. See note 2.

15. See ibid. and note 13.

16. *Principles of Sociology.*

17. *Principles of Sociology.*

18. Herbert Spencer, *Principles of Psychology* (New York: Appleton, 1898, originally published in serial form in 1855).

19. *Principles of Sociology,* p. 3.

ed relations among other animals, such as primates,[20] other mammals, and birds. Sociology is a subscience of super-organic structuring because it analyzes human society that "transcends all others in extent, in complication, and importance."[21]

Spencer saw evolution, or the building of structure, as related to three sets of factors. First, there are environmental factors, such as climate, typography, resources, and other geographic as well as ecological forces. Second, there are the members of a social system themselves whose number, physical traits, emotions, and knowledge can vary. And third, there are "derived factors" that emerge as structure is elaborated. Eventually, such derived factors shape the natures of individuals in society and the environment in which a society exists. The most crucial derived factors are[22] (1) the increasing size of a population and its density in a given environment, (2) the increasing heterogeneity of a population as individuals perform specialized tasks, (3) the increasing productivity of the population as it generates both material and cultural products, (4) the increasing elaboration of government to regulate large, dense, heterogeneous, and productive populations, and (5) the increasing modes of contact, particularly war and commerce, among societies undergoing elaboration of structure. And thus[23]

> the pre-established environing influences, inorganic and organic, which are at first almost unalterable, become more and more altered by the actions of the evolving society. Simple growth of population brings into play fresh causes of transformations that are increasingly important. The influences which the society exerts on the nature of its units, and those which the units exert on the nature of society, incessantly co-operate in creating new elements. As societies progress in size and structure, they work on one another, now by their war-struggles and now by their industrial intercourse, profound metamorphoses. And the ever-accumulating, ever-complicating super-organic products, material and mental, constitute a further set of factors which become more and more influential causes of change.

At this point, Spencer launched into a four-hundred-page analysis of the "original" factors—environment and "primitive" human

---

20. Ibid., p. 7 for an interesting set of insights into primate social organization.
21. Ibid.
22. Ibid., pp. 10-14.
23. Ibid., p. 14.

aggregations—in order to set into context the analysis of derived factors.[24] These four hundred pages are almost always ignored in commentaries on Spencer's work, and yet, they are crucial to overcoming some of the misconceptions about Spencer. I will not dwell on these pages here, because their content is repeated in later chapters on religion (see Chapter 10). But these pages shed light on one crucial point: Spencer's theory of ideas and symbols. Durkheim was particularly critical of Spencer because he interpreted Spencer to overemphasize exchange processes in integrating social structures. But Durkheim did not read, or he chose to ignore, these early pages in *Principles of Sociology*.

In a sense, these pages are Spencer's version of the elementary forms of the religious life.[25] They deal primarily with the first symbol systems and their elaboration into religious ideas that are used to integrate small bands of humans. The discussion is far more detailed than Durkheim's "analysis"[26] of the Arunta aborigines and it contains the same cognitive structuralism found in his and Marcel Mauss's *Primitive Classifications*.[27] Moreover, it draws from a much larger base of ethnographic data (which were to become more formally arrayed in his *Descriptive Sociology;* see Chapter 6).

The conclusion is one that Durkheim drew in *The Division of Labor in Society:* increasing size, differentiation, and productivity changes the cognitive categories of individuals and the nature of their idea systems. As societies initially elaborate, so do the cognitive categories and the number of deities in religious beliefs. But much like Comte[28] argued earlier, there comes a point in the elaboration of structure when rational ideas, such as civil law, become necessary for integration of the larger, more complex and more productive social mass.

There are many errors in this analysis. For example, Spencer argues that language becomes more complex as social structures differentiate, and that intelligence grows with the elaboration of structures. Yet, despite these errors, which are no worse than those made by Durkheim

24. Ibid., pp. 16-446.

25. I will come back to this point in Chapter 8 on Spencer's analysis of "ceremonial instutions" and Chapter 10 on "ecclesiastical institutions."

26. Émile Durkheim, *The Elementary Forms of Religious Life* (New York: Free Press, 1947, originally published in 1912).

27. Émile Durkheim and Marcel Mauss, *Primitive Classifications* (Chicago: University of Chicago Press, 1963, originally published in 1903).

28. Comte, *Positive Philosophy*.

in similar lines of argument, there is a core conclusion: the functions of religious ideas for integrating social structures decrease with increases in population size, social differentiation, and economic productivity, whereas the functions of civil law increase. Moreover, in the closing pages of Part I of *Principles of Sociology,* Spencer stresses that as the functions of cultural ideas decrease, so must the functions of political authority increase. Durkheim did not like this argument for it went against his moral biases and desire for a "civil religion," but the underlying argument is very similar to that in *The Division of Labor.*[29]

I have engaged in this digression into Part I of *Principles of Sociology,* because it is usually ignored. Most secondary analyses of Spencer begin with Part II, which is 447 pages into the work. One almost always sees Chapter 2 of Part II on "society as an organism" represented without the hundreds of pages before and after this chapter; and as a result Spencer's functionalism is given more weight in our retrospective view than it deserves. At the same time, our ignorance of Part I sustains Durkheim's critique that Spencer failed to recognize the functions of ideas. And as a result of this situation, the merits of Spencer's substance analyses of social evolution are typically distorted.

As we turn to Part II of *Principles of Sociology,*[30] then, I will stress the functionalism in his arguments in this chapter, but as we continue with Part II in the next chapter, I will minimize the functional analysis and emphasize the substantive theoretical contribution. This is, after all, what we have done with Durkheim—forgiven the functionalism and focused on the the profound substance. And as I emphasized earlier, in all fairness we should do it for Spencer, especially as most of Durkheim's ideas are anticipated in Spencer's work.[31]

PRINCIPLES OF SOCIOLOGY, PART II: STRUCTURING AND FUNCTION

The Organismic Analogy

The opening chapter of Part II is only two pages, but it makes several points. One anticipates Durkheim's insistence that society be

29. And, I suspect, more accurate than Durkheim's wish for a moral solidarity.

30. *Principles of Sociology,* pp. 447-662. This is the bulk of Spencer's analytical sociology. It is what Spencer is most remembered for; and yet, it constitutes only one hundred and fifty pages of a work that runs over two thousand pages.

31. We must recall that Spencer is writing twenty years earlier than Durkheim.

viewed as "thing" and as an "emergent reality." Indeed, in a way much more forthright than Durkheim, he addressed the realist versus nominalist issue and concludes that we must

> regard a society as an entity, because, though formed of discrete units, a certain concreteness in the aggregate of them is implied by the general persistence of the arrangement among them.[32]

The other major point in this short opening chapter is that society must be regarded as a distinctive level of reality and that its similarities to other realities reside in the underlying principles—that is, his "first principles"—that typify all evolution:[33]

> But now, regarding a society as a thing, what kind of thing must we call it? It seems totally unlike every object with which our senses acquaint us. . . . Between a society and anything else, the only conceivable resemblance must be one due to *parallelism of principle in the arrangement of components.* (italics in original)

This first chapter of Part II represents an important qualification to Chapter 2. As this chapter stresses, super-organic systems do reveal certain "parallel principles" of organization with organic bodies. Unfortunately the chapter title reads "society is an organism" rather than "society reveals certain abstract principles of social organization similar to those of organism"—less catchy title but more in tune with Spencer's true intent. Yet, in seeing this isomorphism between organic and super-organic bodies, it is not hard to see how Spencer would be increasingly drawn into a functional interpretation. When analyzing the elements of inorganic processes—say, the formation of crystals or a solar

32. *Principles of Sociology,* p. 448.

33. Ibid. Indeed, Spencer went to great lengths in his "qualifications and summary" section of Part II to emphasize again that "there exist no analogies between the body politic and a living body, save those necessitated by that mutual dependence of parts which they display." Ibid., p. 592. Moreover, in the footnote to this passage, Spencer notes that:

> This emphatic repudiation of the belief that there is any special analogy between the social organism and the human organism, I have a motive for making. A rude outline of the general conception elaborated in the proceeding eleven chapters, was published in . . . January 1860. In it I expressly rejected the conception of Plato and Hobbes, that there is a likeness between social organization and the organization of a man; saying that "there is no warrant whatever for assuming this."

See also note 8.

system—Spencer was not tempted to delve into "the functions" of these elements for sustaining the emergent whole, but when seeing a close parallel between society and organisms, it is all too easy to begin to argue functionally. Just as a biologist asks about the functions of an organ for the maintenance of the organism, so sociologists begin to inquire into the functions of social structures for the maintenance of society. All functionalism begins with this basic analogy that, throughout the history of social thought, has been introduced many times. But Spencer developed the analogy systematically, and hence, forged functionalism into a clear mode of analysis.

He began in this second chapter of Part II.[34] In this chapter, he outlined the similarities—parallels in principles of organization —between society and organisms as well as some of the critical points of dissimilarity. Let me first review the points of similiarity:[35]

(1) As organic and super-organic bodies increase in size, they increase in structure. That is, they become more complex and differentiated.

(2) Such differentiation of structures is accompanied by differentiation of functions. Each differentiated structure comes to serve distinctive functions for sustaining the "life" of the systemic whole.

(3) Differentiated structures and functions require in both organic and super-organic bodies integration through mutual dependence. Each structure can be sustained only through its dependence upon others for vital substances.

(4) Each differentiation structure in both organic and super-organic bodies is, to a degree, a systemic whole by itself (i.e., organs are composed of cells and societies of groupings of individuals), and thus the larger whole is always influenced by the systemic processes of its constituent parts.

(5) The structures of organic and super-organic bodies can "live on" for a while after the destruction of the systemic whole.

These points of similarity between organisms and society, Spencer argued, must be qualified for their points of "extreme unlikeness."[36]

(1) There are great differences in the degree of connectedness of the parts, or structures, in organic and social wholes. In super-organic wholes, there is less direct and continuous physical contact and more dispersion of parts than in organic bodies.

34. Ibid., pp. 449-622.
35. Ibid., pp. 449-457.
36. Ibid., pp. 457-462.

(2) There are differences in the modes of contact between organic and super-organic systems. In the super-organic, there is much more reliance upon symbols[37] than in the organic.

(3) There are differences in the levels of consciousness and voluntarism of parts in organic and super-organic bodies. All units in society are conscious, goal seeking, and reflective, whereas only one unit can potentially be so in organic bodies.

After drawing this analogy, Spencer went on to stress the first three points of similarity in subsequent chapters. The body of Spencerian theory thus resides in his analysis of how growth, differentiation, and integration in super-organic bodies occur. This analysis continues to analogize back and forth between organic and super-organic systems;[38] and I will try to extract the important substantive principles from this analysis in later chapters. For the present, I want to emphasize how this analogizing led Spencer to a form of analytical functionalism.

Spencer's Analytic Functionalism

As Spencer continued to analyze, he began to develop what I have called "requisite functionalism."[39] Like Parsons and Malinowski, Spencer emphasized that organic and super-organic bodies reveal certain universal requisites that must be fulfilled and that these same requisites exist for all organic and super-organic systems. Let me quote Spencer on this point:[40]

> Close study of the facts shows us another striking parallelism. Organs in animals and organs in societies have internal arrangements framed on the same principle.
>
> Differing from one another as the viscera of a living creature do in many respects, they have several traits in common. Each viscus contains appliances for conveying nutriment to its parts, for bringing it materials on which to operate, for carrying away the product, for draining off waste matters; as also for regulating its activity.

37. Note again how Durkheim in his critique of Spencer in *The Division of Labor* ignored statements like this.

38. But, these principles of organic and super-organic evolution are consistently viewed as derivative of his first principles, which, as we saw in the last chapter, analogizes to the physics of his time.

39. See my *The Structure of Sociological Theory,* 3rd Edition (Homewood, Illinois: Dorsey Press, 1982).

40. *Principles of Sociology,* p. 477.

It is not hard to see the seeds of Talcott Parsons's universal functional requisites in this passage. Indeed, on the next page from this quote, Spencer argued that "it is the same for society" and proceeded to list the basic functional requisites of societies. For example,

> (and) the clustered citizens forming an organ which produces some commodity for national use, or which otherwise satisfies national wants, has within its subservient structures substantially like those of each other organ carrying on each other function . . . It has a set of agencies which bring the raw material . . . ; it has an apparatus of major and minor channels through which the necessities of life are drafted out of the general stocks circulating through the kingdom . . . ; it has appliances . . . for bringing those impulses by which the industry of the place is excited or checked; it has local controlling powers, political and ecclesiastical, by which order is maintained and healthful action furthered.[41]

Although these universal requisites are not as clearly separated as they are by later functionalists, such as Bronislaw Malinowski and Talcott Parsons,[42] the logic of the analysis is clear. First, there are certain universal needs or requisites that social structures function to meet. These revolve around (1) securing and circulating resources, (2) producing usable substances, (3) regulating and integrating internal activities through power and symbols. Second, each system level—group, community, region, or whole society—reveals a similar set of needs. Third, the important dynamics of any empirical system revolve around processes that function to meet these universal requisites. Fourth, the level of adaptation of a social unit to its environment is determined by the extent to which it meets these functional requisites.

Thus, by recognizing that certain basic or universal functions must be met, analysis of organic and super-organic systems is simplified. Although "changes of structure cannot occur without changes of function,"[43] these specific functions can be seen as subclasses of certain basic functional needs. These needs, as Spencer argued in further detail in Chapter 5 of Part II on "social functions,"[44] revolve around needs for integrating differentiated parts, needs for sustaining the parts of

41. Ibid., p. 478.
42. See notes 2 and 13.
43. Ibid., p. 485.
44. Ibid., pp. 485-490.

the system, needs for producing and distributing information and substances, and needs for political regulation and control. In simple systems, these needs are met by each element of the system; but when structures begin to grow and become more complex, they are met by distinctive types of structures that "specialize" in meeting one of these general classes of functions. And, as societies become highly complex, then structures become even more specialized and meet only a subclass of these general functional needs.

The logic behind this form of requisite functionalism guided much of Spencer's substantive analysis. As he began to explore the evolution and structuring of social systems, he sought to identify "systems of organs" that correspond to the basic functional needs of both organic and super-organic bodies. He borrowed from *Principles of Biology* and argued that there arises initially a difference between an "internal" and "external" system. The external system deals with the exigencies of the environment and the internal system with sustaining the operation of the internal parts. Then, as the external and internal "organs" are clearly differentiated, the problems of coordinating the exchanges of substances between the inner and outer organs increase. Thus

> in both the individual and social organisms, after outer and inner systems have been marked off from one another, there begins to arise a third system, lying between the two and facilitating their co-operation. Mutual dependence of the primary-contrasted parts, implies intermediation; and in proportion as they develop, the apparatus for exchanging products and influences must develop too.[45]

From this "biological law," Spencer saw a parallel to the three classes of structures and functions of society; (1) the regulatory, (2) the sustaining, and (3) the distributive. The regulatory are those structures involved in coping with the external environment and in maintaining internal control. The sustaining are those structures that produce human, material, and symbolic resources necessary to maintain individuals as well as the groupings that make up a society. And the distributive are those structures that transmit and transport information, products, people and other resources. Thus, unlike contemporary requisite functionalists who tend to find four universal functions, Spencer finds three, although the issues addressed by Parsons and Spencer are very similar. And, like contemporary functionalists,

45. Ibid., p. 494.

the analysis of social systems proceeds in terms of how structures meet these general classes of needs—that is, regulative, sustaining, and distributive needs.[46]

Just as Parsons analyzed structures and processes primarily with respect to the needs for adaptation, goal attainment, integration and latency, or just as Durkheim studied social arrangements only in relation to the need for social integration, so Spencer began to analyze social phenomena in terms of how they meet needs for regulation, sustenance, and distribution. Yet, even though Spencer classified structures in terms of their analytic functions for the systemic whole, his theoretical ideas are much more readily disassociated from his functionalism than are either Parsons's or Durkheim's modes of functionalism. Let me elaborate on this point, because it bears upon the question of how to salvage substantive theoretical ideas from their functional trappings.

For Parsons, his requisite functionalism became a mode of theoretical explanation. If the functional needs served by a phenomenon can be identified, then it is explained. Such a strategy makes Parsonian functionalism a typological exercise of matching empirical events to one of four analytical needs (as well as the other analytical devices of the Parsonian scheme, such as the "generalized media of exchange" or the "cybernetic hierarchy"). There are, as a result, very few propositions of the sort: "X varies with Y" or "Y is a (mathematical) function of X." And so, there is relatively little theory in Parsons; rather, there is much metatheory but this rarely becomes translated into abstract propositions, law, or principles.

For Durkheim, it is easier to salvage his ideas because explanation involves both causal and functional analysis. His functional analysis is highly moralistic, because Durkheim carried a vision of the "good" and "bad" society. And when he talks about integration, he means the "good" society and when he talks about the "pathologies" of a society, he means "the bad." But his causal analysis saves him, for here one can find statements of covariance that go beyond "Y meets the needs of a society for integration" (i.e., his view of what is good). He also tries to show the causes of Y, and thus his functionalism can be saved because statements like "X causes Y" or "Y is a (mathematical) function of X" can be found.

46. Ibid., pp. 485-548.

Such is even more the case for Spencer. His sociology always seeks to explain how X and Y vary together (and incidentally, can be deduced from his "first principles"). The functional needs are categorizing techniques, as they are for Parsons, but explanation does not consist of determining "the function of X for meeting a system need." Rather, his theoretical analysis is always concerned with demonstrating how variations in regulating, sustaining, and distributing processes are a (mathematical) function of other variables.

In his more descriptive works, however, the three functional requisites do organize his presentation of data. As I have argued elsewhere, such is probably the only use to which we can profitably put functional analysis.[47] By using notions of functional needs as methodological (as opposed to theoretical) criteria for determining important from less important data, we can develop useful descriptions of empirical events. Naturally, it is more desirable to have theoretically based criteria (i.e. axioms, laws, propositions, or principles) for presenting data, but in their absence functionalism is useful. Indeed, I suspect that functionalism gained such favor in the social sciences precisely because we lacked mature social theory at the time that functional analysis came to dominate American sociology and anthropology.

As I will try to document in the next chapter, however, Spencer had a well developed set of theoretical principles that he also used in analyzing data on different societies. And, as I have emphasized, it is relatively easy to separate his functional and theoretical analysis in his descriptive works. Before turning to these descriptive works,[48] which, I should add, constitute the bulk of Spencerian sociology, we need to present Spencer's abstract theoretical ideas disembodied from the functional approach presented in this chapter. For it is in these theoretical ideas that Spencer's enduring contribution to sociology resides.

47. Jonathan H. Turner and Alexandra Maryanski, *Functionalism* (Menlo Park: Benjamin/Cummings, 1978).

48. The bulk of *Principles of Sociology* is descriptive and describes the transformations of institutional structures during societal growth and differentiation. Moreover, we will review Spencer's "descriptive sociology," a multivolume work that he commissioned in order to provide a comprehensive data base for studying social structure.

5

The Analytical Models and Abstract Principles

SPENCER AS A THEORIST

Talcott Parsons's query about "who now reads Spencer" echoed earlier obituaries for Spencer, leaving Parsons to conclude that "Spencer is dead."[1] By the 1950s, funeral orations were commonplace, but in the late 1960s and early 1970s, efforts at resurrection could be found.[2] Evolutionary thinking regained some respectability as issues of development and modernization once again became topical. But the effort at resurrection failed as renewed critiques of evolutionary thinking from both the ideological right[3] and left[4] appeared. And today, with the exception of a few such as the Lenskis' excellent work,[5]

1. Talcott Parsons, *The Structure of Social Action* (New York: McGraw-Hill, 1937), p. 1. As Perrin notes, however, Parsons was echoing the words of the historian Crane Brinton. See Robert G. Perrin, "Herbert Spencer's Four Theories of Social Evolution," *American Journal of Sociology* 81 (May, 1976), p. 1.

2. See Perrin, *Journal of Sociology*.

3. Robert A. Nisbet, *Social Change and History* (New York: Oxford University Press, 1969).

4. For a recent example, see: Anthony Giddens, *A Contemporary Critique of Historical Materialism* (Berkeley, University of California Press, 1981).

5. Gerhard Lenski and Jean Lenski, *Human Societies: An Introduction to Macrosociology* (New York: McGraw-Hill, 1982).

an evolutionary view of history is recessive. In its place is the neo-evolutionism of "world systems theory"[6] and its variants, such as "depending theory."

What is distressing about this failed resuscitation of Spencer is that it revolved around a very narrow interpretation of "evolution." Even those who sought to view Spencer's ideas in a broader context have emphasized the weakest points in Spencer's work—the moral philosophy, the organicism, the unilineal evolutionism, and the functionalism.[7] What they all seem to have ignored is the *theoretical* argument in Spencer's sociology. Spencer viewed "evolution" and "dissolution" as the processes of structuring and destructuring that revolve around growth, differentiation, integration, phases of equilibrium, and disintegration. Granted, he found the processes of growth, differentiation, and integration, and phases of equilibrium more interesting than disintegration, or as he phrased it in *First Principles,* than the process of dissolution. Such is the case with most sociologists today, for we are interested in how structures are created, built-up, sustained, and changed, although we should pay more attention to their dissolution and disintegration.

As I said, we have failed to appreciate Spencer's more purely theoretical work because it has not been untangled from his functionalism and his descriptive evolutionism. I have already addressed his functionalism in the last chapter and I will deal with his descriptive work in the next. Here, I want to treat Spencer as a theorist—as someone who articulated some of sociology's basic laws of human organization. These are not laws of the stages of societal growth from simple to complex, but laws about certain basic and fundamental processes of human organization in general. In fact, as I proceed to outline these laws, they will seem very familiar because they have been rediscovered in a number of subfields in sociology, such as complex organizations, human ecology, and community. His ideas also reappear in some of the classic works of the late nineteenth and early 20th centuries. For example, Émile Durkheim's[8] and Vilfredo Pareto's[9] works both involve restatement of Spencerian theory.

6. See, for example, the two volumes by Immanuel Wallerstein on *The Modern World-System* (Academic Press, 1974 and 1980).

7. See Perrin, *Journal of Sociology,* for example.

8. Émile Durkheim, *The Division of Labor in Society* (New York: Free Press, 1964, originally published in 1893). Indeed, this work is filled with critical references to Spencer, and yet, I think that Durkheim "protests too much" in an effort to hide his borrowing of Spencer's ideas.

9. Vilfredo Pareto, *The Rise and Fall of Elites: An Application of Theoretical Sociology* (Totowa: NJ: Bedminster Press, 1968, originally published in 1901.

My goal in this chapter is to present Spencer's theoretical ideas in a highly abstract way, devoid of the substantive examples in which they are embedded. Most of these examples involve references to organic processes and societal evolution. I will return to the substantive context in the next chapter, but it is important, I feel, to present Spencer's ideas as analytical models and abstract principles. Too often, we have let our ideological reservation about Spencer's moral philosophy and our intellectual qualms about functionalism and evolutionism get in the way of viewing Spencer as a theorist whose ideas have endured (if only by rediscovery).

This exercise may offend some who always insist that we look at ideas in their textual context. As I indicated in my preface to this book, such a view is antithetical to a cumulative science. Moreover, Spencer himself was committed to a deductive view of theory, as these laws of social organization are deductions from his first principles.[10] And so, in pulling out the essential theoretical ideas of Spencer's work, I am merely illustrating the logic behind Spencer's own Synthetic Philosophy, or general systems approach.[11]

THE OVERALL ANALYTICAL MODEL

Spencer saw the process of *social* evolution (structuring), equilibrium (rhythmic phasing), and dissolution (destructuring) as a special case of the more general processes outlined in *First Principles*.[12] Forces in the social universe cause "homogeneous masses" to aggregate or to grow; the "retained motion" of these forces causes differentiation of units through "segregation" into diverse environments and "multiplication of effects." Such differentiation sets into motion processes to generate "integration of matter," leading to increased "coherence" and "defineness" of a "heterogeneous mass." Eventually, this mass reaches equilibrium and reveals "cycles," "phases," and "rhythms" that, over the long run, lead to "dissolution," unless new "forces" in the environment cause further evolution. As Spencer noted in his summary of his long discussion of social evolution:[13]

The many facts contemplated unite in proving that social evolution forms a part of evolution at large. Like evolving aggregates in general, societies

10. Herbert Spencer, *First Principles* (New York: A. C. Burt, 1880, originally published in 1862).

11. See Chapter 3.

12. Ibid.

13. Herbert Spencer, *Principles of Sociology* Volume 1 (New York: Appleton, 1898, originally published in 1874), pp. 596-597.

show *integration,* both by simple increase of mass and by coalescence and re-coalescence of masses. The change from *homogeneity* to *heterogeneity* is multitudinously exemplified; up from the simple tribe, alike in all its parts, to the civilized nation, full of structural and functional unlikeness. With progressing integration and heterogeneity goes increasing *coherence.* We see the wandering group dispersing, dividing, held together by no bonds; the tribe with parts made more coherent by subordination . . . . the cluster of tribes united in a political plexus . . . ; and so up to the civilized nations. Simultaneously comes increasing definiteness. Social organization is at first vague; advance brings settled arrangements which grow slowly more precise; customs pass into laws . . . ; and all constitutions, at first confusedly intermingled, slowly separate, at the same time that each within itself marks off more distinctly its component structures. Thus in all respects is fulfilled the formula of evolution. There is a progress toward greater size, coherence, multiformity, and definiteness. (italics in original)

My point with this long quote is to stress, once again, the continuity in Spencer's analytical work from its beginnings with *First Principles* in 1862 to the mature sociological work in the 1870s. More important, of course, is the underlying model of sociocultural dynamics in Spencer's analysis of evolution. This model is represented in Figure 5.1.

In Figure 5.1, I have rephrased Spencer's ideas somewhat in order to give them a more modern cast. But the ideas remain unchanged. The essence of Spencer theory revolves around the assertion that as systems grow in size, the increased social mass cannot be supported in a given environment without social differentiation. However, differentiation always creates problems of integration, coordination, and control of larger numbers of distinctive units, especially because common cultural symbols (what Spencer termed "sentiments" in a way that anticipated Pareto) can no longer have the same salience for diverse units operating in distinctive environments.[14] Such integrative problems can lead to dissolution of the social mass if they cannot be resolved through the consolidation and centralization of political power as well as through the development of a system of mutual interdependencies of differentiated units. But there is always

14. Durkheim, *Division of Labor,* made a big point about Spencer's unwillingness to talk about morality. However, both Durkheim and Spencer reach the same conclusion: common collective symbols become difficult to sustain in differentiated social systems. See Spencer, *Principles of Sociology,* p. 585.

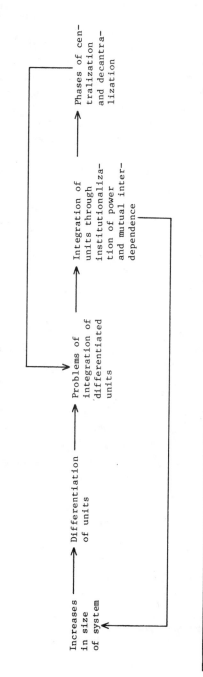

Figure 5.1

a dialectic between these two integrating processes, for if integration is achieved through too much centralization of power, then resistance mounts and pressures build to deregulate system units. Conversely, if deregulation occurs, sustaining linkages among diverse social units increases and, as a result, pressures build for the consolidation of power to control and regulate poorly coordinated activity. And so, differentiated social systems will cycle back and forth between more centralized and decentralized profiles.

Once some degree of integration of a differentiating system is achieved (that is, it does not "dissolve"), then it can increase in size because it now has the structural base to take on more mass (through aggregation of previously unrelated units or through multiplication of existing units). This growth initiates a new phase of differentiation, escalating integrative problems, and their resolution through further consideration of political power and expanded mechanisms for maintaining mutual interdependence. At any point, the system can dissolve as a result of environmental forces or as a result of an inability to implement effective integrative procedures.

If this general scenario sounds like Durkheim in *The Division of Labor*,[15] or any number of more recent works,[16] it is a testimony to how profound were Spencer's insights. As I will document in more detail, Spencer provided sociology with some of its basic laws of organization. We tend to forget these, for reasons that are not clear to me. Maybe it is because Émile Durkheim told us that Spencer was useless (while at the same time borrowing virtually all of Spencerian sociology).[17] Perhaps it was because Talcott Parsons informed us that "Spencer was dead" (while using Spencer's ideas in his own analytical scheme).[18] I really do not know why the original source of these very fundamental ideas has been lost, but I hope in the following pages to rectify this intellectual tragedy by delineating in more detail the elements of Spencer's analytical model.

15. Durkheim, *Division of Labor*.

16. Talcott Parsons, *The System of Modern Societies* (New York: Englewood Cliffs, NJ: Prentice-Hall, 1971).

17. It might be argued, as Durkheim asserted in his "other dissertation," that he took many ideas from Montesquieu's *The Spirit of the Laws* (London: Colonial Press, 1900, originally published in 1748). But I believe that he borrowed even more from Spencer.

18. See note 16.

MODELS AND PRINCIPLES OF SYSTEM GROWTH
AND DIFFERENTIATION

The Analytical Models

Figure 5.2 outlines Spencer's model of the relationship between growth and differentiation in social systems. Social systems can increase in size by two processes: (1) aggregation of previously unrelated units and (2) internal multiplication of units.[19] In either or both cases, a social system will increase in size, which, in turn, creates problems of how to "sustain" each unit. These problems lead to specialization and mutual interdependence of units that exchange services, materials, and resources. Pressures for specialization increase dramatically, Spencer argued, when environmental contrasts are great. If there are limited resources or if members of growing a system are ecologically, politically, or culturally confined to an area,[20] then the increased productivity and efficiency that comes with specialization becomes even more necessary. Spencer emphasized, however, that fission of units (their dispension in space) or dissolution of the system often occurs as a result of growing size. There is no inexorable movement toward specialization and mutual interdependence. Yet if the system is able to sustain itself in an environment, then it will develop independent specialties among its units. Reliance upon specialization creates problems of coordination and control among productive units. Hence if fission or dissolution do not occur, then differentiation of regulatory and operative processes will ensue. That is, specialization will involve the development of distinctive units that have the power to control productive ("operative" or "sustaining" units in Spencer's terminology) activity.[21] As this differentiation occurs, and as regulatory and operative structures internally differentiate, then problems of distribution escalate. These problems create pressures for separate distributive units to emerge.[22]

It is very important to emphasize, as is done in Figure 5.2, that Spencer viewed growth and differentiation as involving numerous

---

19. Spencer, *Principles of Sociology,* pp. 463-471.

20. Note how similar this argument is to Durkheim's notions of "dynamic" and "moral" density in *The Division of Labor.* See Spencer, *Principles of Sociology,* pp. 463-490.

21. Spencer, *Principles of Sociology,* pp. 485-548.

22. Ibid., pp. 494-505.

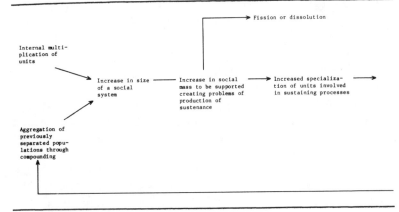

Figure 5.2

critical feedback cycles. Differentiation among regulatory (political), operative (productive and sustaining), and distributive processes creates a structural base for further aggregation of units, which sets into motion those processes that encourage further specialization of units with respect to regulatory, operative, and distributive processes. Within this larger cycle are several critical feedback loops. Differentiation always escalates problems of coordination and control that can cause further differentiation of regulatory structures; or potentially, these problems can also cause the dissolution of the system if such further differentiation does not occur. If differentiation of distinctive distribution processes develop, then this allows for further differentiation of regulatory and operative processes; and conversely, if separate distributive processes (markets, generalized media such as money, communication networks, transport systems, etc.) cannot emerge, then further differentiation and aggregation will be difficult.[23] Also, differentiation of operative, regulatory, and distributive structures increases reliance upon mutual interdependence, which, in turn encourages further differentiation of these structures. At any point, of course, the system can dissolve if growth creates problems of production, coordination, control, and distribution that cannot be resolved.

Thus social evolution involves a situation where these feedback loops are all positive. That is, specialization and differentiation along

23. Note again how these feedback cycles become prominent "causes" of "dynamic density" in Durkheim, *Division of Labor*.

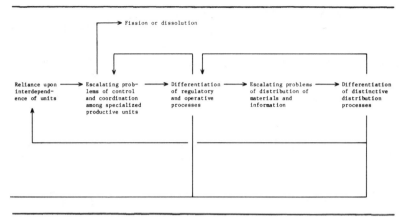

Figure 5.2 Continued

regulatory, operative, and distributive axes resolve problems of production, coordination, control, and distribution in ways that encourage further increases in size and differentiation. As Spencer made these arguments, he had a vision of societal evolution from simple hunting and gathering societies to industrial societies. But his principles are, I think, applicable to any system referent. If systems grow, they differentiate along the lines specified in Figure 5.2.

This model has been used primarily in contemporary organizational theory, but it has been used in the study of other units, such as small groups, urban ecology, and governments. Most of these more recent efforts appear unaware of Spencer's work of one hundred years ago. Yet even a cursory comparison of their models with Spencer's reveals how Spencerian they are. For example, Peter Blau's[24] well-known model of differentiation in organizations essentially applies to Spencerian ideas to complex organizations. Size produces structural differentiation in organizations at decelerating rates; structural differentiation enlarges the adminstrative component of organizations; and problems of coordination and control among differentiated units eventually place a lid upon organization growth. I am not asserting, of course, that Blau's and others' work in this area does not represent considerable refinement of Spencer's ideas. But I am arguing that these

24. Peter M. Blau, "A Formal Theory of Differentiation in Organizations," *American Sociological Review* 35 (April, 1970), pp. 201-218.

refinements are merely corollaries to abstract principles first developed by Spencer. To take other examples of recent research: Abrahamson's[25] finding that political complexity is positively correlated with system size, complexity, and threat is a confirmation of Spencerian principles; Noell's[26] analysis of the positive relationship between the size of state government and the complexity of the broader social structure in a state is another confirmation of Spencer's ideas; Stephan's[27] study of the relation between growth and county government represents yet another interesting application of Spencer; Karsada's[28] finding the growth of the periphery of metropolitan areas influences the political centralization of the area similarly confirms Spencer's theoretical ideas; Hannan's and Freeman's[29] analysis of population growth, resource scarcity, and organizational differentiation likewise confirms Spencer's propositions; Goldman's[30] confirmation that organization size and complexity are related and that distributive functions (communication networks) are a critical intervening variable on political centralization represents another test of Spencer's model; Anderson's[31] finding that organization size and administrative complexity are related in a sample of hospitals further confirms Spencer's basic laws; Gibbs' and Browning's[32] analysis of size, technology, and the division of labor is distinctly Spencerian; Labovitz's and Miller's[33] study of research organization also confirms Spencer's model about size, differentiation,

25. Mark Abrahamson, "Correlates of Political Complexity," *American Sociological Review* 34 (October, 1969), pp. 690-701.

26. James J. Noell, "On the Administrative Sector of Social Systems: An Analysis of the Size and Complexity of Government Bureaucracies in American States," *Social Forces* 52 (June, 1974), pp. 549-558.

27. G. Edward Stephen, "Variation in County Size: A Theory of Segmental Growth," *American Sociological Review* 36 (June, 1971), pp. 451-461.

28. John D. Kasarda, "The Theory of Ecological Expansion: An Empirical Test," *Social Forces* 51 (December 1972), pp. 165-176.

29. Michael T. Hannan and John H. Freeman, "The Population Ecology of Organizations," *American Journal of Sociology* 82 (March, 1977), pp. 929-964.

30. Paul Goldman, "Size and Differentiation in Organizations," *Pacific Sociological Review* 16 (January 1973), pp. 89-106.

31. Theodore R. Anderson, "Organization Size and Functional Complexity," *American Sociological Review* 26 (February, 1961), pp. 23-27.

32. Jack P. Gibbs and Harley L. Browning, "The Division of Labor, Technology, and the Organization of Production in Twelve Countries," *American Sociological Review* 31 (February 1966), pp. 81-93.

33. Sanford Labovitz and Jon Miller, "Implications of Power, Conflict, and Change in an Organizational Setting," *Pacific Sociological Review* 17 (April 1974), pp. 214-239.

and centralization of authority; the Scott's[34] comparison of small group structures uncovers that role differentiation and centralization of leadership are related in a way predicted by Spencer's model; and so on. I do not want to belabor the general point here, which is: A great deal of empirical work has been unknowingly testing out the implications of Spencerian sociology. The only problem is that most of those who have done this research seem unaware of Spencer. They have, in essence, rediscovered Spencer. Again, I am not saying that these researchers have not added to Spencer's legacy, but I do believe that if they had been aware of Spencer's principles, they could have contributed even more to cumulation of theory in sociology.

One way to document the extent to which Spencer's theoretical ideas are being used in contemporary sociology is to extract the abstract proposition in Spencer's thought. Such an exercise gives us a more refined view of Spencerian sociology.[35] Indeed, the models in Figures 5.1 and 5.2 only provide an outline of the general categories in his theoretical ideas. They do not tell us in very precise ways the nature of relations among the variables specified in these categories. Moreover, Spencer argued in propositional form, not in analytical models. He did so because he viewed his "principles of sociology" as theorems to his "first principles." I am, therefore, much closer to Spencer's intent by presenting Spencer's ideas on growth and differentiation as statements of covariance.

The Abstract Principles

In outlining Spencer's ideas on size and differentiation in social systems, I will begin with his principle on the causes of social differentiation.[36]

> *Principle 1:* The degree of social differentiation among members of a population is a positive additive function of (a) the absolute

34. William A. Scott and Ruth Scott, "Intercorrelations Among Structural Properties of Primary Groups," *Journal of Personality and Social Psychology* 41 (August, 1981), pp. 279-292.

35. I have made such efforts in a number of places. See Leonard Beeghley's and my *The Emergence of Sociological Theory* (Homewood, Illinois: Dorsey Press, 1981), pp. 108-113; my "The Forgotten Giant: Herbert Spencer's Theoretical Models and Principles," Revue Europeene Des Sciences Sociales, XIX (59, 1981), pp. 79-98; and for a comparison of Durkheim's principles from *The Division of Labor* and those developed twenty years earlier by Spencer, see my "Durkheim's and Spencer's Principles of Social Organization: A Theoretical Note," *Sociological Perspectives* 27 (January 1984), pp. 21-32.

36. Spencer, *Principles of Sociology,* pp. 463-470.

size of the population; (b) the level of resource scarcity in the environment of the population; (c) the degree of ecological concentration of the population; and (d) the level of integration among previous differentiations among members of the population.

As I have documented elsewhere,[37] Emile Durkheim[38] is often given credit for these ideas, as are more recent theorists such as Blau.[39] Let me review each element in the proposition to specify further Spencer's ideas. For Spencer, structural differentiation must accompany increases in population size, because as the social mass grows, there must be a more complex structure to sustain this larger mass.[40] In the organic universe, this is achieved by skeletal and physiological complexity, whereas in the super-organic realm, this occurs through the elaboration of the division of labor. Resource scarcity increases the pressures for the division of labor because it escalates competition over resources, and hence, forces social units to specialize if they are to survive.[41] Ecological concentration further increases these competitive pressures because social units cannot disperse in an effort to survive; instead, they must find specialized niches. Differentiation cannot proceed, however, if previously generated differences are not well integrated through links of mutual interdependence, through established patterns of distribution, and through political regulation. For if existing patterns of differentiation are not integrated, then growth, resource scarcity, and ecological concentration will create competitive pressures that dissolve the system.[42]

37. See my "Durkheim's and Spencer's Principles."

38. Durkheim, *Division of Labor.*

39. See notes 24-34.

40. This is a basic engineering principle that, as a self-trained civil engineer, Spencer knew well. He applied this principle to his work in biology (where it is still used today) and then adapted it for super-organic systems.

41. Actually, Durkheim, *Division of Labor,* pp. 265-266, uses the "struggle for existence" mechanism much more prominently than Spencer. Durkheim saw the division of labor as caused by competition in ecologically dense situations revealing dynamic density. He even makes reference to Darwin's "law" on selection. Spencer's model is far less "tooth and claw" in its emphasis on individual competition. Indeed, Durkheim takes a position that is usually attributed (unfairly) to Spencer.

42. A view that Durkheim, in contrast to Spencer, could not bring himself to recognize. Again, Spencer is much more likely than Durkheim to acknowledge the disintegration of social systems.

The next principle on growth and differentiation concerns the form and pattern structural differentiation, once it is initiated.[43]

> *Principle 2:* The greater the pressures for social differentiation among members of a population (Principle 1), the greater are the pressures for initial differentiation between, and elaboration of, regulatory (political) and operative (sustaining) structures, followed by the differentiation and elaboration of distinctive distributive structures.

This principle states Spencer's conviction that differentiation runs along three axes. One involves the emergence of structures to regulate, control, and coordinate the activities of other structures. Such regulatory structures are political because they involve the use of power to regulate. Without them, differentiation becomes chaotic because there is no "force" to bind diverse units together. Although ideas (symbols) can bind very simple systems together[44] and although mutual dependence can integrate diverse units, cultural (symbolic) unity is difficult to sustain during differentiation, whereas interdependence cannot, by itself, fully integrate diverse units. There must be a regulatory agent to replace the functions of idea systems and to enforce, coordinate, and control relations of mutual dependence. I suspect that, contrary to Durkheim's critique of Spencer and his fervent hope for symbolic unity in differentiated systems (in order to avoid anomie), Spencer was closer to the truth.[45] At best, ideas can only provide broad symbolic frameworks; the real work of integration is provided by the differentiation of separate political centers that regulate processes of mutual interdependence among system units.

By operative or sustaining structures, Spencer denoted the non-regulatory, internal processes of a social system that produce material and human resources for the sustenance of the system. These become distinct from regulatory structures and internally differentiated (for example, in societal evolution, economy and kinship become

---

43. Spencer, *Principles of Sociology,* pp. 471-497 for the general discussion. Then, from pp. 498-548, Spencer analyzes each of these three "subsystems" in more detail.

44. Contrary to Durkheim's portrayal and our often distorted views of Spencer, he recognized the significance of cultural symbols is simple (noncomplex) systems. But he recognized better than Durkheim that "political force" was critical to integration in complex systems.

45. Although Spencer is labeled the laissez-faire ideologue (he was, but not in his sociology), Durkheim is the one, in my view, who underemphasizes power. Spencer is much closer to Marx and Weber in his stress on the significance of political power in social system dynamics.

differentiated; as do resource extraction and production; as do education and kinship; and so on). As the volume of transactions among
these operative structures increases, so must their political regulation.

Eventually, this growing volume of transactions within and between
operative and regulatory structures escalates problems of distribution
to a point where distinctive structures for distribution of material,
symbolic, and human resources emerge and elaborate. At the societal
level of organization, markets and related structure emerge; and
transportation systems expand; media and communication networks
increase in importance. And so, differentiation involves a tri-part
split of structures as regulatory, operative, or distributive.[46]

The next set of principles state Spencer's views on the generic
conditions that increase (or decrease) the elaboration and internal
differentiation of regulatory, operative, and distributive structures.
The first principle in this set states the conditions increasing political
regulation of operative and distributive processes:

> *Principle 3:* The degree of elaboration and differentiation of the regulatory
> capacity in a social system is a positive and additive function
> of: (a) the level of external threat;[47] (b) the degree of internal
> dissimilarity and inequality;[48] (c) the total volume of trans-
> actions and complexity of networks;[49] and (d) the level of
> productivity.[50]

One of the critical variables in almost all of Spencer's is war
and conflict.[51] War or the threat of war with other societies causes
the consolidation and centralization of political power in order to
mobilize, coordinate, and regulate human and material sources to
pursue conflict. I have phrased this variable more abstractly as
"external threat" to a system, but this rephrasing is consistent with
Spencer's intent. Another central variable in Spencer's sociology—
one which is rarely appreciated by his critics—is the "internal threats"
caused by dissimilarity of social units and by inequalities. If social units

---

46. See, for a nice summary statement, Spencer, *Principles of Sociology*, p. 595.
47. Ibid. pp. 519, 543, 579, 581.
48. Ibid., p. 571.
49. Ibid., pp. 547, 595.
50. Ibid., pp. 532-533.
51. Indeed, in almost every discussion of social processes, war and conflict are
the central variables. In later chapters, where I will extract empirical generalizations
from Spencer's substantive analysis, this fact will become increasingly evident.

are dissimilar (in terms of ethnicity, religion, culture), then their interests (goals and purposes) can often come into conflict. Similarly, if there is great inequality, the interests of those with and without resources vary and there is a constant potential for conflict. Such potential for conflict, whether the result of dissimilarity or inequality,[52] forces centralization or regulatory power to control conflict.

The other variables causing centralization of power are interrelated. As systems become more differentiated, the volume of internal transactions and the complexity of social networks increases. Without some degree of external regulation and control by centers of power, chaos ensues; and thus, social systems that evidence complex networks and a high volume of transactions will be more centralized than those with simple networks and a low volume of internal transactions. Increased productivity increases both differentiation of social networks and the volume of transactions, but it also operates as an independent force in centralization of power. As the economy grows, it requires political control because normal entrepreneurial mechanisms for pooling land, labor, and capital are inadequate, because the infrastructural requirements of high productivity (such as regulation of money and contracts) are beyond the capacity of nongovernmental sectors to meet, and because the distributive problems (markets and transportation) increase to a point where regulation is necessary. I have phrased these variables more abstractly than Spencer did (as he was primarily interested in societal level processes), but the intent is the same: Centralization of power is a partial function of productivity and the volume of internal transactions.

This proposition runs counter to the inaccurate stereotypes about Spencer sociology, but this is his argument. Granted, he preferred a relatively decentralized government; and he believed that societies revealing high productivity and high levels of internal transactions will remain comparatively decentralized. But if external and internal threats also exist, then centralization of power will increase dramatically.[53] Thus Spencer gave much more weight to the conflict variables than the others in his theoretical analysis. Indeed, Spencer was very much a conflict theorist, for as we see in later chapters, his analysis of society

52. Spencer, *Principles of Sociology,* p. 510.
53. Indeed, Spencer opposed English colonization, precisely because it created a condition of external threat, and hence, political centralization.

always examines the relationship between power and conflict potential in social systems.

> *Principle 4:* The degree of elaboration and differentiation of operative processes in a social system is a positive function of productivity, with the level of productivity being a positive and additive function of (a) the availability of resources, (b) the level of technology, and (c) the differentiation of distinctive distributive structures, while being a curvilinear function of (d) the differentiation of regulatory centers.

In this principle,[54] Spencer argues that those processes sustaining the units of a social system become differentiated and more elaborated as the level of productivity increases. In turn productivity is related to resource levels in the environment and the technological knowledge base of the system. Equally important, productivity cannot increase without clear differentiation of regulatory centers and distributive processes. For otherwise, any increase in production will be thwarted by inadequate coordination and distribution of human and material resources. Yet this relationship is curvilinear, as excessive regulation thwarts the expression of operative processes (see Principle 6 below).

> *Principle 5:* The degree of elaboration and differentiation of distributive processes is a curvilinear function of the differentiation of regulatory centers and a positive function of the differentiation of operative processes.

Spencer felt that there is lag in the differentiation of distributive from operative processes.[55] It is only after operative processes have developed considerably that problems of circulation of resources escalate to the point where distinctive distributive processes emerge. Similarly, without regulatory centers to coordinate and control distribution, it cannot expand. But this relationship is curvilinear: Initial increases in regulatory control increase distributive processes, but very high levels of regulation thwart the emergence of diverse distributive structures.

These five principles summarize, at the most abstract level, Spencer's analysis of growth and differentiation in super-organic systems. The principles add considerably to the model present in Figure 5.2, because they specify variables and relations among these variables. Moreover,

---

54. Spencer, *Principles of Sociology,* pp. 498-501.
55. Ibid., p. 494.

they highlight aspects of Spencer's work that are not given sufficient attention in most commentaries. Let me mention some of these. First, contrary to the portrayal of Spencer as a knee-jerk ideologue for laissez-faire (which he was *when doing moral philosophy*), his sociology emphasizes the structural inevitability of concentrated power. Secondly, contrary to views of Spencer as a conservative organicist and functionalist, the principles stress the significance of conflict (both external and internal) to social systems. And third, as I will now discuss in more detail, there is a dialectical mode of analysis in Spencer's discussion of power in social systems.

MODELS AND PRINCIPLES OF POLITICAL DIALECTICS

The Analytical Model

In Figure 5.3, I have outlined Spencer's model on the inherent dialectic of political regulation. As I will discuss in more substantive detail in the next chapter, Spencer's ideas on this dialectic are contained in his discussion of "militant" and "industrial" types of societies.[56] In contradiction to many commentaries on this dichotomy, Spencer did not view this distinction as a necessary evolutionary sequence, but rather, as a variation in the degree of political centralization or decentralization in a social system.[57] Philosophically, he preferred decentralized (industrial) systems, but he recognized that political centralization (militant) is a fact of social life in all types of systems, from very simple to complex ones. "Industrial" does not denote a mode of production, but rather, the degree to which operative and distributive processes are free from extensive political regulation. "Militant" does denote military organization to pursue conflict, but it also describes the regulation of operative and distributive processes by political authority.

The critical point in Spencer's model is that centralized power sets into motion forces that bring about decentralization. Conversely, decentralized power generates conditions that cause the centralization of power. There is, then, an inherent dialectic in political regulation. Politically centralized systems create pressures for their decen-

56. Ibid., pp. 549-587.
57. He hoped that it would be an evolutionary sequence; and indeed, in the postscript to Part II, he began to assert that "industrial types" were the highest form of evolution. But in the original text, this evolutionism is not evident. See Ibid., p. 599.

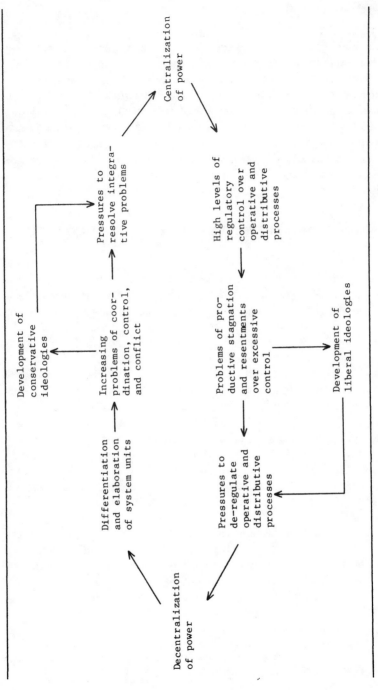

Figure 5.3

tralization, and vice versa. As is evident, Spencer's model anticipates that developed later by Vilfredo Pareto.[58] Indeed, the argument is virtually the same as Pareto's: Decentralized power allows for growth, elaboration, and differentiation of units; such elaboration and differentiation increase problems of coordination and control; these problems create conservative "sentiments" (Spencer's actual term), or ideologies emphasizing conformity, control, and order, that along with integrative problems themselves generate pressures to centralize power; centralization of power involves extensive regulation of activities, which, over time, stagnates production and generates resentments; these resentments cause liberal ideologies emphasizing individual freedom from constraint to emerge, and along with the structural problems of stagnation, generate pressures for decentralization of power.

Social systems cycle back and forth in this way; and this fact, Spencer argued, can be seen as further confirmation that there is a rhythmic quality to evolving systems that are approaching their equilibrium point (see Chapter 3 on first principles). Moreover, as we will see in subsequent chapters where we examine Spencer's analysis of social institutions, the structural profile of institutions like kinship, religion, law, and ceremony is greatly circumscribed by the degree of political centralization versus decentralization. Indeed, it becomes the major explanatory variable in Spencer's descriptive work—far more central than the evolutionary sequence so commonly seen as the key element of Spencerian sociology.

The Abstract Principles

We can complete this overview of Spencer's dialectic by translating the elements in the model present in Figure 5.4 into abstract propositions that can be viewed as important supplements to those principles already presented.

> *Principle 6:* The pressures for centralization of regulatory processes in a social system are an additive and positive function of (a) the degree of unrestricted elaboration and differentiation of operative and distributive processes, (b) the duration of their unrestricted elaboration, (c) the level of conservative ideological mobilization, and (d) the degree of external and internal threat.

58. Pareto, *The Rise and Fall of Elites.*

As is evident, we can introduce more variables by converting the model in Figure 5.3 to a proposition. Of particular importance, as I noted earlier, is the level of external threat (conflict with other systems) and internal threat (conflict and tension among system units).[59] As Principle 3 emphasized, these are the major conditions for differentiation and elaboration of regulatory processes; and thus it is not surprising that they are also conditions for centralization of such regulation. But even without these external and internal sources of threat, the dialectical processes outlined in the model also operate. That is, prolonged and unrestricted elaboration of system processes create integrative problems and conservative ideologies, all of which, in turn, generate pressures for centralization. In a sense, these integrative problems are a major source of "internal threat," especially if inequalities are great.

Principle 7: The pressures for decentralization of regulatory processes in a social system are an additive and positive function of (a) the degree of restrictive control of operative and distributive pressures, (b) the duration of this restriction, (c) the level of liberal ideological mobilization, while being an inverse function of (d) external and internal threat.

This principle states the converse of those conditions listed in Principle 6, but they pose some interesting implications. For example, a highly centralized system creates its own pressures for decentralization, but if the level of external or internal threat suddenly decreases, then these processes are dramatically increased. Yet, as Spencer worried, centralized power is difficult to dismantle (especially war machines), even under the pressures of overregulation and stagnation. And so efforts on the part of political elites to find "new enemies" are often undertaken to counter the structural and ideological pressures for decentralization, hence, the loss of their power. Thus depending on the respective weights of the variables listed in Principles 6 and 7, the pressures for centralization or decentralization can vary.

THE THEORETICAL LEGACY AND THE LOST PROMISE

The models and principles presented in this chapter summarize much of Spencer's theoretical legacy. I should note that in these principles

59. Spencer, *Principles of Sociology,* pp. 571-579.

one does not find very much in the way of laissez-faire ideology, functionalism, organicism, and other points of emphasis attributed to Spencer. Spencer was all of these things—an ideologue, a functionalist, an organicist—but his sociology is written so that these deficiencies can be easily ignored. The ideology is very easy to ignore, because it hardly appears in Spencer's sociology. And yet, so many just assume that Spencerian sociology is riddled with references to "survival of the fittest" and ideological tracks on the virtues of laissez-faire. This is just not the case. The functionalism is very evident but it is confined to the short chapters at the beginning of Part II of Volume I and to tracing the origins of social institutions. The organicism is obvious because Spencer always draws a parallel to organisms and societies, but the comparison is merely for illustrative purposes. And thus the models and principles are easy to extract; indeed, they hit you between the eyes without burdening the reader with ideology, functionalism, and organicism.

Probably what is most evident in Part II of Volume I, where most of Spencer's major theoretical ideas appear, is the enormous range of ethnographic data presented to document points. Not only did Spencer illustrate with examples from biology,[60] he also provided examples from ethnographic sources. And, as one moves further into *Principles of Sociology,* these data become more and more evident. In fact, one gets a hint in Part I of *Principles of Sociology* of what is to come in later Parts of this multivolume work. In a sense, Part II is a relatively brief theoretical interlude in a very ethnographic treatise. Yet, as I will document shortly, Spencer's use of ethnographic examples is almost always for a more theoretical purpose.

A really critical question that is rarely asked about these examples used to illustrate Spencer's theoretical ideas is this: Where did he get so much descriptive information? Before we complete a review of *Principles of Sociology,* we need to answer this question. Spencer left social science with more than a series of theoretical principles; he also initiated a major effort at cross-cultural data collection in an effort to create a data base for testing more theoretical ideas. It is a great tragedy that this portion of Spencer's work is even more ignored than his analytical and theoretical work. For most of Spencer's theoretical ideas have been rediscovered, but his data base has been lost forever.

---

60. After all, he wrote *Principles of Biology* (New York: Appleton, 1864-1867) before he embarked on the study of super-organic systems.

Moreover, the strategy that he proposed for arranging data for purposes of comparison was lost in a time when anthropology needed it desperately, before traditional societies were lost forever and completely.

The loss of enduring theoretical ideas is, perhaps, less burdensome. It merely slows the process of theory cumulation. In the end, the theoretical principles had to be rediscovered because they are so fundamental. But the loss of a data base on types of societies that were fast disappearing and the ignorance of his strategy, which only much later was to be used by George Murdock in his Human Relations Area File, represent even a more grievous loss. I want to pause and consider this loss in the next chapter, before returning to the rest of *Principles of Sociology.*

6

Spencer's Human Relations Area Files

Spencer developed three different approaches for summarizing the vast amounts of ethnographic and historical data that appear in his works. One approach is the one most often identified with Spencer: evolutionism. For although Spencer used the term "evolution" to denote the more generic process of structuring, he also employed the term in the traditional sense: stages of societal development from simple to complex. Much of the data on different types of societies are thus arrayed in a way to describe the stages of societal evolution from simple hunters and gatherers through horticulture and agriculture to modern industrial systems. Another approach for summarizing data revolves around the cyclical phases of societies from centralized ("militant") to a more decentralized profile ("industrial" in the general sense of relatively unregulated operation of sustaining processes). The third approach, which has been almost completely lost, involves developing broad analytical categories for describing processes in all types of societies.

In this chapter, I will examine each of these approaches. I will first examine Spencer's evolutionary or stage model of societal development. Next, I will explore the cyclical model on movement from militant to industrial, and vice versa. And finally, I will explore in detail what is perhaps the most interesting approach: the effort to create human relations area files for cross-societal comparison.[1]

SPENCER'S DESCRIPTIVE MODEL OF SOCIETAL EVOLUTION

Spencer viewed societal evolution as a process of growth and differentiation along three axes: the regulative, the operative or sustaining, and the distributive. Growth can occur by internal increases in the size of a population, but Spencer placed more weight on successive compounding or aggregating of smaller "social masses" to form a larger one. He felt that this process of compounding is basic to growth in both organic and super-organic (societal) bodies.[2]

So that in both organic and super-organic growths, we see a process or compounding and recompounding carried to various stages. In both cases, after some consolidation of the smallest aggregates there comes the process of forming larger aggregates by unions of them; and in both cases repetition of this process makes secondary aggregates into tertiary ones.

Or, as he summarized at the end of Part II in Volume I of *Principles of Sociology*:[3]

We saw that societies are aggregates which grow; that in the various types of them there are great varieties in the growths reached; that types of successively larger sizes result from the aggregation and re-aggregation of those small sizes; and that this increase by coalescence, joined with interstitial increase, is the process through which have been formed the vast civilized nations.

As a result of this emphasis on compounding (typically through war and conquest but also through political alliances), Spencer's stages

---

1. I have deliberately used George Murdock's terms, because the intent of Spencer's system is the same as Murdock's. There is, no doubt, of some connection between Murdock and Spencer, because William Graham Sumner and Albert Keller, who borrowed from Spencer, were Murdock's teachers. See George P. Murdock and others' *Outline of Cultural Materials* (New Haven: Human Area Relations Files, 1961). See also his "The Cross-Cultural Survey," *American Sociological Review* 5 (March, 1940), pp. 361-370.

2. Herbert Spencer, *Principles of Sociology* (New York: Appleton, 1898, originally published in 1874-1876), p. 469 of Volume 1.

3. Ibid., p. 593.

of evolution are phrased in terms of the degree of compounding. He lists five basic stages: simple without leaders, simple with leaders, compound, double compound, and treble compound. These correspond roughly to evolutionary models that classify societies in terms of their mode of economic production: hunting and gathering, simple horticulture, advanced horticulture, agriculture, and industrial. For each of these types, except the industrial, which he felt was obvious to all of his readers, he provided tabular and descriptive summaries.[4] In Table 6.1, I have reconstructed these summaries in a way that includes the treble compound (modern industrial) and that also adds information to the tabular presentation data from his more discursive comments.[5]

As can be seen from Table 6.1, Spencer described each stage of societal evolution in terms of the structure of regulatory, operative, and distributive processes as well as the demographic profile of the society. I would submit that this classification, presented in 1874, is as sophisticated as any presented in more recent analyses and that it is an extremely accurate description of the types of societies that have typified humans' evolutionary history. I do not propose to defend a rigid view of unilineal evolution, or to become bogged down in the many criticisms of evolutionary thinking. But we cannot deny that human societies have changed in the pattern presented in Table 6.1. Moreover, if we compare this description with any of Spencer's approximate contemporaries in the last century—Marx, Weber, Durkheim, Tyler, Morgan, for example—there can be no doubt that Spencer's is the most detailed and the most accurate.

Another way to visualize Spencer's argument is in terms of a model of (a) growth through compounding, (b) successive differentiation of regulatory, operative, and distributive structures, and (c) increasing internal differentiation of the structures falling within these three axes. In Figure 6.1, I have summarized the data from Table 6.1 in a way that represents his view of growth and differentiation.

Table 6.1 and Figure 6.1 thus represent the approach to summarizing ethnographic and historical data. By viewing societies in terms of their stage of evolutionary development (or their degree of compounding) and by arguing that each stage reveals a particular profile of structures with respect to regulatory, operative, and distributive processes, vast amounts of data can be given coherence and order. This has always

(text continues on page 92)

4. Ibid., p. 551-559.
5. This table is adapted from Leonard Beeghley's and my *The Emergence of Sociological Theory* (Homewood, Illinois: Dorsey Press, 1981), pp. 92-93.

TABLE 6.1

	Simple Society		Compound Society	Double Compound	Treble Compound (never formally listed)
	Headless	Headed			
Regulatory System	temporary leaders who emerge in response to particular problems	permanent chief and various lieutenants	hierarchy of chiefs, with paramount chief, local chiefs, and varieties of lieutenants	elaboration of political state; bureaucratized; differentiation between administration	modern political state
Operative System:					
Economic structure	hunting and gathering	pastoral; simple agriculture	agricultural; general and local division of labor	agriculture; extensive division of labor	industrial capitalism
Religious structure	individualized religious worship	beginnings of religious specialists: shaman	established ecclesiastical arrangements	ecclesiastical hierarchy; rigid rituals and religious observance	religious diversity in separate church structures
Family structure	simple; sexual division of labor	large, complex; sexual and political division of labor	large, complex; numerous sexual, age, and political divisions	large, complex; numerous sexual, age, and political divisions	small, simple; decrease in sexual division of labor
Artistic-literary forms	little art; no literature	some art; no literature	artists	artists; literary specialists; scholars	many artistic literary specialists; scholars
Law-customs	informal codes of conduct	informal codes of conduct	informal codes; enforced by political elites and community members	positive law and codes; written	elaborate legal codes; civil and criminal

Community structure	small bands of wandering families	small, settled groupings of families	village; permanent buildings	large towns; permanent structures	cities, towns, and hamlets
Stratification	none	chief and followers	five or six clear ranks	castes; rigid divisions	classes; less rigid
Distributive System:					
Materials	sharing within family and band	intra- and inter-familial exchange and sharing	travel and trade between villages	roads among towns; considerable travel and exchange; traders and other specialists	roads, rail, and other non-manual transport; many specialists
Information	oral, personal	oral, personal	oral, personal; at times, mediated by elites or travelers	oral; written; edicts; oracles; teachers and other communications specialists	oral, written, formal media structures for edicts; many communications specialists
Demographic Profile:					
Size	small	larger	larger; joining of several simple societies	large	large
Mobility	mobile within territory	less mobile, frequently tied to territory	less mobility; ties to territory; movement among villages of a defined territory	settled; much travel among towns	settled; growing urban concentrations; much travel; movement from rural to urban centers

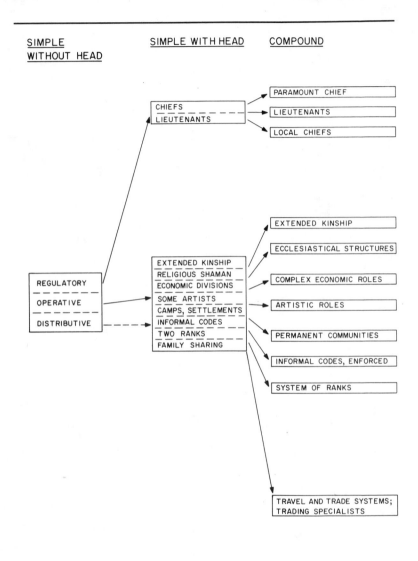

Figure 6.1

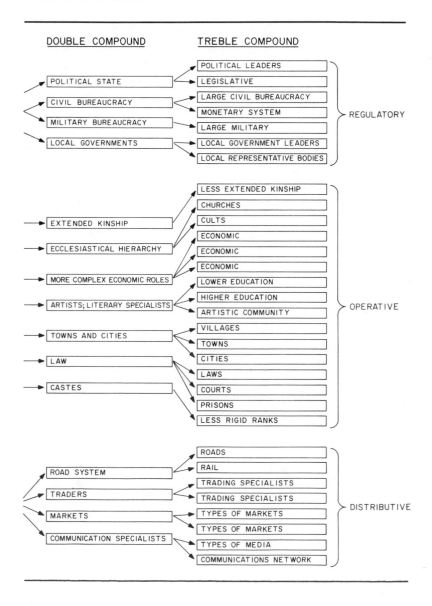

DOUBLE COMPOUND   TREBLE COMPOUND

POLITICAL STATE → POLITICAL LEADERS
                 → LEGISLATIVE

CIVIL BUREAUCRACY → LARGE CIVIL BUREAUCRACY
                    MONETARY SYSTEM

MILITARY BUREAUCRACY → LARGE MILITARY

LOCAL GOVERNMENTS → LOCAL GOVERNMENT LEADERS
                    → LOCAL REPRESENTATIVE BODIES   } REGULATORY

EXTENDED KINSHIP → LESS EXTENDED KINSHIP
                   CHURCHES
                   CULTS

ECCLESIASTICAL HIERARCHY → ECONOMIC
                           ECONOMIC
                           ECONOMIC

MORE COMPLEX ECONOMIC ROLES → LOWER EDUCATION
                              HIGHER EDUCATION

ARTISTS; LITERARY SPECIALISTS → ARTISTIC COMMUNITY
                                VILLAGES

TOWNS AND CITIES → TOWNS
                   CITIES

LAW → LAWS
      COURTS

CASTES → PRISONS
         LESS RIGID RANKS   } OPERATIVE

ROAD SYSTEM → ROADS
              RAIL

TRADERS → TRADING SPECIALISTS
          TRADING SPECIALISTS

MARKETS → TYPES OF MARKETS
          TYPES OF MARKETS

COMMUNICATION SPECIALISTS → TYPES OF MEDIA
                            COMMUNICATIONS NETWORK   } DISTRIBUTIVE

been the appeal of evolutionary thinking; and Spencer was the first to present the data in a sophisticated evolutionary model. Surprisingly, in the 1960s and 1970s, when evolutionary thought made a bit of a comeback in the social sciences,[6] Spencer is hardly mentioned, even though his work was the most thorough and detailed of the original evolutionary models.

SPENCER'S DESCRIPTIVE MODEL OF POLITICAL DIALECTICS

Spencer's second classificatory scheme is more analytical than his evolutionary model. The reason for this shift in the level of abstraction is that relatively simple or complex societies can be either politically centralized or decentralized. Indeed, as Principle 5 and Principle 6 presented in the last chapter document (see also Figure 5.3), social systems tend to cycle back and forth between militant (politically centralized) and industrial (politically decentralized) states. And so, if compound as well as trebly compound (see Figure 6.1) societies can be either "militant" or "industrial" (in the sense of being decentralized politically), the typology must be stated at a level of abstraction that encompasses both simple and complex system. Thus, in addition to classifying a society by its stage of development, it is also possible—and in fact, necessary—to classify it as either militant or industrial. As Spencer emphasized:[7]

> We class societies, then, in two ways; both having to be kept in mind when interpreting social phenomena.
>
> First, they have to be arranged in the order of their integration, as simple, compound, doubly-compared, trebly-compared.... Much less definite is the division to be made among societies according as one or the other of the great systems of organs is supreme. Omitting the lowest types which show no differentiations at all, we have but few exceptions to the rule that each society has structures for carrying on conflicts ... and for carrying on sustenations; and as the ratios between

6. See, for example, Gerhard Lenski, *Power and Privilege: A Theory of Stratification* (New York: Mcgraw-Hill, 1966) and *Sociology: An Introduction to Macro Sociology* (New York: McGraw-Hill, 1970); Talcott Parsons, *Societies: Evolutionary and Comparative Perspectives* (Englewood Cliffs, NJ: Prentice-Hall, 1966) and *The System of Modern Societies* (Englewood Cliffs, NJ, Prentice-Hall, 1971).

7. Spencer, *Principles of Sociology,* p. 574.

these admit of all gradation, it results that no specific classification can be based on their relative developments. Nevertheless, as the militant type, characterized by predominance of the one, is framed on the principle of compulsory co-operation while the industrial type, characterized by predominance of the other, is framed on the principle of voluntary cooperation, the two types, when evolved to their extreme forms, are dramatically opposed; and the contrasts between their traits are among the most important with which Sociology has to deal.

I want to draw attention to this last sentence because as will become increasingly evident, the relative dominance of regulatory or operative processes is a far more critical variable in Spencerian sociology than the descriptive model of evolution. Although Spencer was interested in the substantive characteristics of simple, compound, doubly-compound, and the trebly-compound societies, he makes much more use of the distinction between militant and industrial profiles in social systems. Principles 6 and 7 in the last chapter give us a sense for the theoretical importance of this distinction between centralized and decentralized forms; and in the next chapters, we will see how crucial this distinction is for more descriptive accounts of ceremony, kinship, politics, religion, economics, and other basic structures of human societies.

Thus, for Spencer, to adequately describe a society we need to (1) determine its stage of development (simple, compound, doubly-compound, and trebly-compound or decentralization). The militant-industrial distinction is not, therefore, an evolutionary classification, as some authors have argued. Rather, it is a way to fine-tune the description of a society, whatever its stage of evolutionary development.

In Table 6.2, I have summarized the analytical elements in Spencer's distinction between militant and industrial societies.[8] The label, "militant," is reasonably unambiguous because such societies are politically centralized and exercise tight control of operative and distributive processes to maintain a defense or to fight wars. The term "industrial" has a more ambiguous meaning because it denotes the predominance of operative and sustaining processes rather than a particular mode of economic production (such as industrial capitalism). This ambiguity has led some to believe that Spencer viewed movement from a militant to industrial profile as an evolutionary sequence, but the distinc-

---

8. This table adapted from Turner and Beeghley, *Sociological Theory,* p. 89.

TABLE 6.2

Basic System Processes	Militant	Industrial
Regulatory Processes		
Societal goals	defense and war	internal productivity and provision of services
Political organization	centralized; authoritarian	less centralization; less direct authority on system units
Operative Processes		
Individuals	high degrees of control by state; high levels of stratification	freedom from extensive controls by state; less stratification
Social structures	coordinated to meet politically established goals of war and defense	coordinated to facilitate each structure's expansion and growth
Distributive Processes		
Flow of materials	from organizations to state; from state to individuals and other social units	from organizations to other units and individuals
Flow of information	from state to individuals	both individuals to state and state to individuals

tion is applicable to a society at any compound stage of evolution. Morally and philosophically, Spencer preferred the decentralized, "industrial" form, but sociologically, he recognized that the militant profile is pervasive in all stages of evolution.

Table 6.3 presents this two-pronged approach to societal classification in visual form. The structure and processes of a society will be very different depending not only on its stage of development but also on its degree of militancy or industrialism. Any description of a society must, therefore, array the data to reveal its stage of evolution and its degree of militancy or industrialism. Almost all of Spencerian sociology implicitly performs this two-step process of classification.

TABLE 6.3   Spencer's Approach to Societal Classification

| | | Describe Phase in Political Cycle | |
		Militant	Industrial
Evolutionary Stage	simple, with head		
	compound		
	double-compound		
	treble-compound		

SPENCER'S HUMAN RELATIONS AREA FILES[9]

Spencer's third approach for arraying ethnographic and historical data is, I feel, the most important. And yet, very few social scientists are aware of it; and in fact, it is even hard to find these data in research libraries of the world. This ignorance of Spencer's *Descriptive Sociology* marks an intellectual tragedy of enormous proportions because, had his strategy been followed, sociology and anthropology would have a much better data base for conducting cross-cultural research.

What was Spencer's *Descriptive Sociology?* Basically, it was an effort to develop some general categories for cataloguing historical (if available) and ethnographic data on diverse types of societies, from the simplest to the most complex. Spencer felt that if he could create a general and comprehensive set of categories, these would guide researchers in the recording of data. Moreover, because the categories are the same for all types of societies, it becomes possible to compare societies in a systematic way. As Spencer noted in the preface to one of the volumes of *Descriptive Sociology:*[10]

In preparation for *The Principles of Sociology,* requiring as bases of induction large accumulations of data, fitly arranged for comparison, I, in October, 1867, commenced by proxy, the collection and organization of facts presented by societies of different types, past and pre-

9. See note 1.
10. *No. 3: Descriptive Sociology; or, Groups of Sociological Facts,* Classified and Arranged by Herbert Spencer, compiled and abstracted by David Duncan (London: Williams and Norgate, 1874).

sent: being fortunate enough to secure the services of gentlemen competent to carry on the process in the way I wished. Though this classified compilation of materials was entered upon solely to facilitate my own work; yet, after having brought the mode of classification to a satisfactory form, and after having had some of the Tables fill up (with data), I decided to have the undertaking executed with a view to publication: the facts collected and arranged for easy reference and convenient study of their relations, being so presented, apart from hypothesis, as to aid all students of Social Science in testing such conclusions as they have drawn and in drawing others.

In all, there were fifteen volumes of *Descriptive Sociology*.[11] The volumes employed a category scheme developed by Spencer, but the actual compilation of the data from diverse sources was done by others. Upon his death, Spencer left sufficient money in his will to have additional volumes completed. And so, several volumes of *Descriptive Sociology* were completed after Spencer's death. This was possible not only because of Spencer's bequest of money to the project, but more importantly, because later editors had very clear guidance from Spencer's system of categories.

The volumes of *Descriptive Sociology* are oversized productions; and almost all open with a tabular presentation of the data. The tabular presentation runs across at least two-faced pages (very large pages indeed, as the volumes are so oversized). If several societies are to be examined in volume, then this open-faced presentation is repeated for each society. There are only slight variations in these tabular presentations of data, which, of course, should be expected as the whole idea of *Descriptive Sociology* is to sustain a common system of classification. The major variation is the addition of subcategories for more complex societies, but these subcategories always fall under more

---

11. The list of volumes of *Descriptive Sociology* is as follows: (1) *English* (1873); (2) *Ancient Mexicans, Central Americans, Chibchans, Ancient Peruvians* (1874); (3) *Types of Lowest Races, Negritto, and Malayo-Polynesian Races* (1874); (4) *African Races* (1875); (5) *Asiatic Races* (1876); (6) *North and South American Races* (1878); (7) *Hebrews and Phoenicians* (1880); (8) *French* (1881); (9) *Chinese* (1910); (10) *Hellenic Greeks* (1928); (13) *Mesopotamia* (1929); (14) *African Races* (1930); and (15) *Ancient Romans* (1934). A revised edition of number 3, edited by D. Duncan and H. Tedder, was published in 1925; a second edition of number 6 appeared in 1885; number 14 is a redoing by Emil Torday of number 4. In addition to these volumes, which are in folio size, two unnumbered works appeared: Ruben Long, *The Sociology of Islam*, 2 vols. (1931-1933), and John Garstang, *The Heritage of Solomon: An Historical Introduction to the Sociology of Ancient Palestine* (1934).

general categories used to portray simpler societies. The basic rationale for this procedure is best summarized by Spencer:[12]

> In further explanation I may say that the classified compilations and digests of materials to be thus brought together under the title *Descriptive Sociology* are intended to supply the student of Social Science with data standing towards his conclusions in a relation like that in which accounts of the structures and functions of different types of animals stand to the conclusions of the Biologist. Until these had been such systematic descriptions of different kinds of organisms, as made it possible to compare the connexions, and forms, and actions, and modes of origin, of their parts, the Science of Life could make no progress. And in like manner, before there can be reached in Sociology generalizations having a certainty making them worthy to be called scientific, there must be definite accounts of the institutions and actions of societies of various types, and in various stages of evolution, so arranged as to furnish the means of readily ascertaining what social phenomena are habitually associated.

Thus, for Spencer, *Descriptive Sociology* is to be much like the Linnean classification system in Biology. By classifying the features of different societies under common categories, it will be possible to see what "social phenomena are habitually associated" and thereby make generalizations about the operation of societies. In Figure 6.2, I have extracted the tabular format, and hence the categories, from number 3 in the series that is very much like all of the other volumes. I have not included the data, but the blank areas (remember the pages in volumes are perhaps as much as eight times larger than the ones in this book) are where descriptions under each category would be written. In a sense, the categories and their tabular organization represent a checklist, forcing the compiler to describe structures and processes in a society for each heading and subheading. Let me now review some of the key features of the tabular form and the underlying category system.

At the top of the table is a short summary of the inorganic environment (geology, topography, and climate), the organic environment (vegetable and animal life), the sociological environment (past history, contacts with distant societies, past societies from which current ones evolved, present neighbors), physical characteristics of the population (skin color, height, weight, hair, teeth, strength, etc.), emotional

12. *Descriptive Sociology,* Number 3, preface.

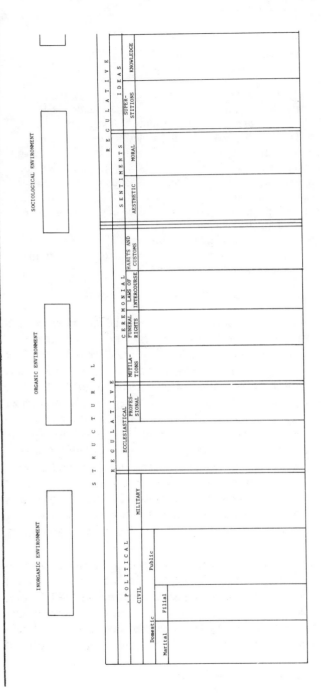

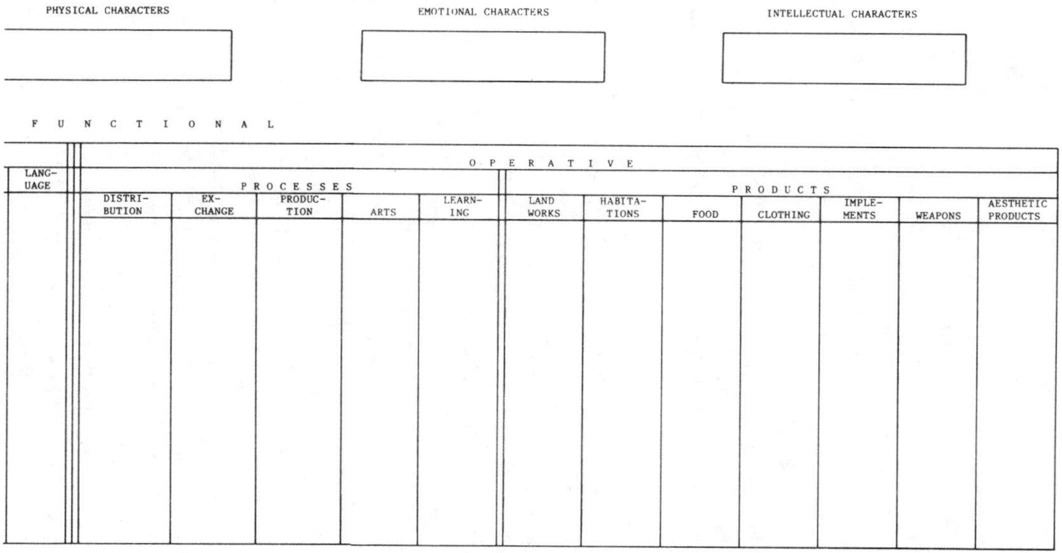
PHYSICAL CHARACTERS
EMOTIONAL CHARACTERS
INTELLECTUAL CHARACTERS
F U N C T I O N A L
O P E R A T I V E
LANG-UAGE
P R O C E S S E S
DISTRI-BUTION
EX-CHANGE
PRODUC-TION
ARTS
LEARN-ING
P R O D U C T S
LAND WORKS
HABITA-TIONS
FOOD
CLOTHING
IMPLE-MENTS
WEAPONS
AESTHETIC PRODUCTS

Figure 6.2

characteristics of the people (e.g., gregariousness, aggressiveness, shyness), and intellectual characteristic of the population (e.g., curiosity, memory, ingenuity, etc.). The descriptions of the inorganic, organic, and sociological environments are typically accurate and useful, but the summaries of the characteristics of the people suffer from evaluative overtones. Such is especially the case when describing non-Western populations. Part of the problem is that these descriptions draw upon accounts of travelers, traders, colonial administrators, ministers, and other nonprofessionals, most of whom were convinced of their own superiority and who tended to look at the physical and behavioral patterns of non-Western peoples through very biased eyeglasses. But the description of the physical, organic, and sociological environments are reasonably objective and useful.

The main body of the chart is the columns filled with brief summaries (they are left empty, in Figure 6.2). The two major categories are between "structural" and "functional," which do not seem to make much sense. They do not follow from his discussion of function in *Principles of Sociology* and can, I feel, be ignored. The next subdivision is between regulative and operative; and here, we can see how this diversion follows from his more theoretical concerns. And, if we ignore the structural and functional division and simply run together the two regulative divisions (one under structural and another under functional), then the data are arranged under two general categories, regulative and operative.

Under regulative, Spencer creates six categories (at least in Volume 3 on primitive societies): political, ecclesiastical, ceremonial, sentiments, ideas, and language. As will become more evident in the next chapter, where we take up Spencer's general discussion of such topics, Spencer saw ceremony (rituals, titles, badges, forms of address, and the like) as essentially regulatory; they *control* interaction and social relations. Also, unlike Durkheim's[13] portrayal of Spencer, Spencer was very much concerned with how symbols to regulate action. Note that the description of sentiments, ideas, and language all appear under regulative. Thus, symbols as they manifest themselves in different forms— sentiments, ideas, and language—are very prominent in Spencer's system of regulatory processes. The more obvious regulatory structures—polity, law, religion—are also prominent but no more so than these symbolic processes.

13. Émile Durkheim, *The Division of Labor in Society* (New York: Free Press, 1947, originally published in 1893).

Under the operative processes, Spencer subdivides this general category into processes and products. In Number 3 of the series, the process of distribution is not given the prominence of other volumes in more complex societies (as the distribution systems of the simple societies in Number 3 are not elaborate). Similarly, other categories (exchange and production) are not extensive because of the types of societies being explored in Number 3. These and other categories do not change, however. Rather, the volumes become wider and filled with more material, but their place in the classificatory scheme remains much the same in all of the fifteen volumes.

In these tabular presentations, there is an explicit strategy for analysis. In Spencer's words:[14]

> Respecting the tabulation, devised for the purpose of exhibiting social phenomena in a convenient way, let me add that the primary aim has been so to present them that their relations of simultaneity and succession may be seen at one view. As used for delineating uncivilized societies, concerning which have no records, the tabular form serves only to display the various social traits as they are found to co-exist. But as used for delineating societies having known histories, the tabular form is so employed as to exhibit not only the connexions (sic) of phenomena existing at the same time, but also the connexions (sic) of the phenomena that succeed one another. By reading horizontally across a Table at any period, there may be gained a knowledge of the traits of all orders displayed by a society at that period; while by reading down each column, there may be gained a knowledge of the modifications which each trait, structural or functional, underwent during successive periods.

I can illustrate this strategy further by comparing Volume Number 1 on "The English"[15] and Number 3 on "Types of Lowest Races." In Number 3, there are successive tables on seventeen different societies: Fuegians, Andamans, Veddahs, Australians (aborigines), Tasmanians, New Caledonians, New Guinea people, Fijians, Sandwich Islanders, Tahitians, Tongans, Samoans, New Zealanders (aborigines), Dyaks, Javans, Sumatrans, and Malagasy. By reading across each table, one can see the structural affinities within a society. By reading down a column for all, or some portion of, the seventeen societies, one can compare societies for that trait. Moreover, because the societies are

14. *Descriptive Sociology,* Number 3, preface.
15. See note 11.

grouped by geographical areas (at least approximately), successive tables represent societies on proximate geographical regions. As these societies do not have a written history, only one table per society is possible. In contrast, the volume on "The English" has successive tables for just one society, as it is possible to trace its history. Thus Number 1 reveals successive tables for prominent historical epochs for one society. Thus reading across the table reveals the affinities of traits for a given historical period, whereas reading down any column offers an overview of the changes in that trait over time.

I have dwelled on Spencer's *Descriptive Sociology* because our typical ignorance of its existence signals the loss of an intellectual resource by twentieth-century anthropologists and sociologists. One consequence of losing Spencer's work is that over fifty years of cross-cultural collection of data was lost. It was not until the 1930s that George Murdock[16] resurrected this kind of approach; but during the intervening years, many of the traditional societies about which we would like to know more were either destroyed or significantly changed by extensive outside contact. If we had only used Spencer's categories to record the accounts of travelers, missionaries, and the emerging ethnographers, we would today have a much better cumulative ethnographic record.

A second consequence is that when systematic ethnographies by professionals actually began to be written in the second decade of the century, most could have profited from a checkpoint like the one contained in Spencer's charts. Save from Bronislaw Malinowski's work on the Trobriand Islanders and Lloyd Warner's study of the Murgin, ethnographies are piecemeal, unsystematic, and not very useful. They suffer from an analytical failure: to have some conceptual scheme to guide the recording of details. With few exceptions, the ethnographies do not give us a very complete view of a society; and I would argue that if they had Spencer's categories as a guide, the ethnographies of this century would be dramatically improved. We would know more about diverse population; and we would have data that could be used for comparative analysis.

Anthropologists are now suspicious of the comparative method. This suspicion is, I think, an admission that their ethnographies are seriously flawed. There is also a bias against cross-cultural work that stems from an excessive relativism (i.e., all societies and cultures are unique) and

16. See note 1.

from a basically antagonistic view to developing general theories from the comparison of human populations. But I think that much of this is merely a cover for the fact that, despite Murdock's efforts to resurrect Spencer's strategy, the data are insufficient to the task. Most admit this, but fail to see why such is the case: the failure to impose some system of categories on data collection and reporting. They had, I feel, a very good set of categories as early as 1874. It is a tragedy that it was never used.

A third consequence of failing to use Spencer's scheme is that, as contradictory as this statement may initially seem, it led to an excessive reliance on *explanatory* functionalism. As ethnographers tried to find coherence in their data and to interpret facts, they were drawn to functional explanations: trait x functions to meet need y in the system. As I have argued elsewhere,[17] the demise of early evolutionism and diffusionism, coupled with the fact that most populations studied by anthropologists had no history, led to an explanatory crisis in anthropology: how to explain events in a culture when one could no longer view them as evidence of a evolutionary sequence, when one could no longer see them as diffused products from "cradles of civilization," and when one could not even trace their history? The answer was anthropological functionalism: that x exists because it meets y need in society. My point is that if anthropology had used functionalism not as an explanatory tool but as a *descriptive* tool, it would have been much better off. Correspondingly, sociology would have avoided its functional dark ages, because had not the anthropologists kept functionalism alive in the first half of the century, functional theorizing would, I think, have died. As a theoretical explanation, functionalism is seriously and fatally flawed; but as a descriptive tool it has some merit. Let me elaborate on this point.

Functionalism asks a very interesting question: What does a society need to survive? Functionalists then create lists of functional needs or requisites that are not particularly useful in explaining *why* and *how* cultural traits exist in a society. But these functional needs are, I think, useful assumptions that can be used to construct guidelines for what is important to observe in a society. For Spencer, there are functional needs for regulation, operation, and distribution in a society; and hence, they become the analytical criteria for his classification scheme. He then asks: What are the basic ways these needs are met? And his

17. Jonathan H. Turner and Alexandria Maryanski, *Functionalism* (Menlo Park: Benjamin-Cummings, 1979).

answer is the various subcategories portrayed in Figure 6.2. Thus functional reasoning often leads to very useful systems of categories that can serve as a checklist for recording important (as defined by functional criteria) events.

But anthropology, and later sociology, did not use functionalism in this way. Rather, it was used increasingly to explain empirical events, despite the fact that it is much better at providing criteria for describing "more important" from "less important" events. This is what the scheme in Spencer's *Descriptive Sociology* does; and had social scientists been more aware of it, they could have realized functionalism's utility as a descriptive tool and perhaps avoided its pitfalls as an explanatory approach.

THE LOST LEGACY:
SUMMARY AND PREVIEW

As I have emphasized, Spencer's three strategies for arraying historical and ethnographic data have been ignored. The overall result is that much of his work had to be rediscovered, wasting a good deal of intellectual energy. Moreover, the timing of this loss and subsequent rediscovery was at a critical point in history when the societies about which we would now like to know more were fast disappearing or losing what was left of their pristine qualities.

Spencer did not have good data; but despite this fact, he did construct a very sophisticated evolutionary model and he did develop a useful system for categorizing sociological data. The reason that his efforts on this score are so good, even by today's standards, is because they are theoretically informed. Spencer had the abstract principles summarized in the last chapter to guide him, as well as his functionalism (see Chapter 4). Just as these principles were lost to social theory, so his descriptive work was ignored by the first generations of anthropologists.

The least useful of Spencer's classificatory schemes is the "militant-industrial" distinction. But curiously, along with Spencer's functionalism it is the most frequently cited portion of his work—yet one more indication of how distorted is our contemporary view of Spencerian sociology. The general idea is interesting and important—political centralization versus decentralization—but as a descriptive tool it does not add much to Spencer's other two approaches, the evolutionary model and the categories of *Descriptive Sociology*. Yet, it is the critical variable in his descriptions of those structures and processes that appear as major categories in *Descriptive Sociology*. Most of *Principles of Sociology* consists of descriptions about the nature, functions, and variations in domestic institutions (Part III), ceremonial institutions (Part IV), political institutions (Part V), ecclesiastical institutions (Part VI), professional institutions (Part VII), and industrial institutions (Part VIII). Although the evolutionary model is used to describe the changes in these institutional complexes, the militant-industrial distinction is the major explanatory variable for understanding the structure and operation of these institutions. And so, with this preview, we can turn to a review of Spencer's analysis of the basic institutional complexes of society.

7

The Creation of Society

Spencer on Domestic Institutions

SPENCER ON INSTITUTIONAL ANALYSIS
IN GENERAL

Two-thirds of *Principles of Sociology*[1] is devoted to an analysis of "institutions." Spencer begins with a discussion of "domestic institutions," or in more modern terms, kinship structures. He then turns to a review of "ceremonial institutions," or what today we might see as micro-interactive analysis. And successively, he examines "political," "ecclesiastical" (religious), "professional," and "industrial" (economic) institutions. By "institutional," Spencer denotes those more enduring structures that meet fundamental functional requisites of human organization and that regulate, control, and circumscribe the actions of individuals and groups in a society.[2]

In this institutional analysis, three points of emphasis can be found. First of all, his analysis is functional, because he often remarks that to "understand how an organization originated and developed, it is requisite to understand the need subserved at the outset and

1. Herbert Spencer, *Principles of Sociology* (New York: Appleton, 1898, orginally initiated in 1874 and completed in 1896).

2. Actually, Spencer never really offers a definition of institutions; and so, I have developed this one on the basis of my reading of him.

afterwards."[3] And at times, he goes so far as to list the functions of an institution.

Yet, having emphasized his functionalism, several important qualifications need to be inserted. The functional statements do not dominate his analysis; and in fact, they can at times seem somewhat extraneous to the line of argument. And much more important, many of the functional statements are, in reality, a shorthand way to phrase a more extensive "group selection" scenario. Spencer's famous phrase "survival of the fittest," for which he has been so resoundedly condemned, is actually a way to summarize conflict and war among *societies*. That is, those structural or institutional features that promote the survival of a population in conflict with other populations are likely to be retained, as they are likely to prevail in a conflict. Contrary to William Graham Sumner's[4] misrepresentation of Spencer, and many commentators since, Spencer's use of this phrase in his sociological works typically concerns the selective pressures that war and conflict between societies generate for certain kinds of structural arrangements within a society. Evolution proceeds by conflict, conquest, and retention of those structural features that facilitated a society's survival. Selection is not so much at the *individual* level, but at the societal level. For example, in his analysis of political institutions, he argues:[5]

> We must recognize the truth that the struggles for existence between societies have been instrumental to their evolution. Neither the consolidation and re-consolidation of small groups into large ones; nor the organization of such compound and doubly compound groups . . . would have been possible without inter-tribal and international conflicts. Social cooperation is initiated by joint defense and offense; and from the cooperation thus initiated, all kinds of cooperations have arisen.

Similarly, other institutional complexes are "selected" in conflict with other societies and in struggles to adapt patterns of social organization to varying environments. The concept of "function" is often used, as

3. Spencer, *Principles of Sociology,* p. 3 of Volume 3.
4. Sumner is, I feel, largely responsible for our view of Spencer as a "social Darwinist." Actually, Darwin is a "biological Spencerian," if anything, but the critical point is that Spencer normally emphasized selection at the *societal* not the individual level. It is Sumner who argued at the individual level. See, for example, William Graham Sumner, *What Social Classes Owe Each Other* (New York: Harper & Row, 1883).
5. Spencer, *Principles of Sociology,* p. 241 of Volume 2.

it is in biology, to summarize in an abbreviated way these selective processes.

This line of argument is buttressed by the second point of emphasis in his discussion of institutional complexes: evolution. His concern is with tracing the evolutionary orgins of an institution in terms of the first selective advantages that it provided a population. In this way, Spencer's functionalism is quite legitimate and avoids many of the problems of functional analysis, because he does not merely construct an ad hoc list of functional needs and then just assert how different structures meet these needs. Rather, he tries to document historically how a given structure provided a selective advantage for a population in a given environment. And only after he has done this task does he describe the elaboration of the structure during evolution. As he does so, the functional statements virtually disappear and the discussion simply tries to summarize with vast amounts of data the evolutionary sequence.

His presentation of an evolutionary sequence does, however, contain an important qualification: Evolution reveals a cumulative direction among societies (as dictated by his law of evolution and first principles), but for any one society, or grouping of societies, a step-by-step sequence cannot be easily found. As he stressed for political evolution:[6]

> if each society grew and unfolded itself without the intrusion of additional factors, interpretation would be relatively easy; but the complicated processes of development are frequently re-complicated by changes in the sets of factors ... In many cases the repeated overrunnings of societies by one another, the minglings of peoples and institutions, the breakings up and re-aggregations, so destroy the continuity of normal processes as to make it extremely difficult, if not impossible, to draw conclusions (about evolutionary sequences).

Thus, although Spencer's analysis of institutions is evolutionary in the gross sense of tracing the overall movement from simple to complex forms of organization, it is not a naive unilineal argument. Moreover, it is much more of an evolutionary argument in the other sense of Spencer's use of this term. That is, he was most interested in how institutional structures are constructed and elaborated. And at times,

6. Ibid., pp. 242-243.

he also discussed dissolution or destructuring of an institutional complex.

This conclusion is supported by the third and most prominent point of emphasis in his discussion of institutions. Spencer was clearly much more interested in explaining variations in the form of an institution than in either recounting its functions or historical evolution. As I mentioned at the end of the last chapter, the elements in the "militant-industrial" dichotomy are the major explanatory variables in understanding the structure of an institution. His emphasis of function and evolution is, in reality, more descriptive than explanatory. For when he really wanted to explain *why* and *how* an institutional complex reveals a particular pattern, the elements of the militant-industrial distinction are invoked far more than references to functions or evolutionary stages.

I have dwelled on these three points of emphasis in Spencer's institutional analysis to overcome well-entrenched biases against Spencer's work. For this and the next chapters, I will illustrate how he actually went about the analysis of social institutions. In this analysis, a number of interesting generalizations that are still useful exist.

SPENCER ON DOMESTIC INSTITUTIONS[7]

Spencer's discussion of kinship can be divided into several inter-related topics: (1) the emergence of kinship among early humans, (2) the historical evolution of kinship structures, and (3) the forces behind variation in kinship. I will develop each of these points in the following sections. In so doing, I will illustrate the general thrust of Spencer's functionalism, his evolutionism, and his use of the militant-industrial distinction as a major explanatory variable.

The Emergence of Kinship

Spencer begins with kinship because it was the first human institution. The rationale for this conclusion is that kinship emerged because

7. As best as I can determine, this portion of *Principles of Sociology,* pp. 603-776 of Volume 1 (or Part III in editions with different volume numbers) was written in 1876, and perhaps extending into early 1877.

it provided selective advantage for human reproduction. Indeed, reproduction is for Spencer the basic functional need of all species:[8]

> Of every species it is undeniable that individuals which die must be replaced by new individuals, or the species as a whole must die. No less obvious is it that if the death-rate in a species is high, the rate of multiplication must be high, and conversely. This proportioning of reproduction to mortality is requisite for mankind as for every other kind.[9]

Thus the basic need is not just reproduction, per se, but a "proportioning" of reproduction so that a species remains adapted to the resource levels of its environment. To "proportion" reproduction requires some degree of regulation of the reproductive process. Species that cannot regulate reproduction are, therefore, "less fit" to survive. And so, there are selection pressures for regulation of reproduction through organic (genetic) or super-organic (organizational) mechanisms.

It is with these assumptions that Spencer criticized the popular notion of his time that "promiscuity" typified early human sexual relations. For Spencer, the existence of humans presupposes some degree of reproductive success that can only be achieved through the regulation of reproduction through organizational mechanisms. True, there must have been a time when there were unions of the sexes, and hence reproduction, that were relatively unregulated by social structure, but such unions would pose serious problems.[10] One set of problems would concern the raising of children by the female in poorly organized groups where promiscuity prevailed. Another problem would revolve around the conflicts and tensions among males over access to females. And so, very early there were "selective pressures" for some degree of regulation of sexual relations as well as for protection and care of children.[11] That is, those societies that could develop more permanent bonds between males and females, while providing safe contexts for

8. Spencer, *Principles of Sociology,* p. 603 of Volume 1.

9. Indeed, Spencer provided a very contemporary discussion of infanticide among hunters and gatherers as a way of maintaining "this proportioning." See Spencer, *Principles of Sociology,* pp. 610-611 of Volume 1.

10. Ibid., pp. 643-653 presents a rather sophisticated set of hypotheses on "promiscuity" among early humans.

11. Ibid., p. 628 for the more detailed argument.

the rearing of children, would be more likely to survive than those that did not. For

> under ordinary conditions the rearing of more numerous and stronger offspring must have been favoured by more regular sexual relations, there must, on the average, have been a tendency for the societies most characterized by promiscuity to disappear before those less characterized by it.[12]

Spencer even speculated that there is "a good deal of evidence . . . that among primates inferior to man, there are monogamic relations of the sexes having some persistence." And he then wondered "why, then, . . . did there come divergences from this arrangement prompted by innate tendencies?" The answer is always couched in terms of a selection process: there had to have been selection pressures in the environments of both humans and nonhuman primates for non-monogamous forms of kinship to evolve out of early monogamy. Thus both the emergence and subsequent evolution of kinship structures are to be explained by selection pressures.

The Evolution of Kinship Structures

Spencer's discussion of the development of kinship structures initially examines patterns of exogamy and endogamy. Then, it turns to an analysis of polyandry, polygyny, and monogamy. In focusing on marriage patterns rather than descent, Spencer's analysis becomes flawed. He clearly understood something about descent systems, for he talks about them in the context of his analysis of marriage rules. But he failed to see that descent is probably more critical than marriage rules for understanding the structure and evolution of kinship structures. Yet, even with this emphasis on marriage, his presentation is nonetheless interesting and, in part, still very useful. The basic line of argument is that the structuring of kinship promotes social integration—sexual, political, and religious.[13] Such integration increases the chances that a society can survive in an environment. For without a kinship system:[14]

> Family bonds . . . are not only weak but cannot spread far; and this implies defect of cohesion among members of the society. Though they have some common interests, with some vague notion of general kin-

12. Ibid., p. 652.
13. Ibid., p. 685.
14. Ibid., p. 649.

ship, there lacks that element of strength arising from interests within groups distinctly related by blood. At the same time, establishment of subordination is hindered. Nothing beyond temporary predominance of the stronger is likely to arise in the absence of definite descent:[15] there can be no settled political control. For the like reason the growth of ancestor-worship, and of the religious bonds resulting from it, are impeded. Thus in several ways indefinite sexual relations hinder social self-preservation and social evolution.

For Spencer, then, kinship has the function of (read as selective advantage for) creating social integration by (1) providing for a stable environment for the raising of children, (2) allowing for social cohesion among kindred, (3) providing for a system of political control, and (4) contributing to religious worship of ancestors. These four selective advantages are the underlying dynamic of Spencer's specific account of marriage patterns. I will begin with Spencer's discussion of exogamy and endogamy, and then, turn to the analysis of plural marriage (and indirectly, descent).

Exogamy and Endogamy. Spencer's general position is that rules of exogamy (marriage must occur outside one's group) and endogamy (marriage must occur inside one's group or a designated outside group) emerge because they facilitate social integration among members of various groupings. Unfortunately, Spencer's analysis is the victim of bad data, for he concludes that endogamy promotes peace between societies by preventing "wife-stealing," whereas exogamy encourages "wife-stealing" and exists under conditions of conflict between societies.[16] But, despite these flaws, his general conclusion anticipates later work by anthropologists; that is, the regulation of where and from whom marriage partners are taken promotes social integration among societies and hence, promotes the continued survival of those societies.

Polyandry and Polygyny. Spencer argued that "irregular relations of the sexes are thus at variance with the welfare of the society,

15. Note here he recognizes the importance of descent, and yet, it is only mentioned in the context of marriage patterns.

16. Spencer overemphasized traditional population's view of women as "property" who were bought, sold, stolen, and taken as prizes of victory in war. And so, he fails to recognize that exogamy can indeed promote political integration when selection of marriage partners is less violent. Yet, his recognition of the basis of male dominance, Spencer, *Principles of Sociology,* p. 675 of Volume 1, is still quite insightful.

of young, and the adults.[17] For as a society comes to regulate its internal affairs, it is better able to compete against other societies:[18]

> The struggle for existence between societies conduces the same effect (stable marriage)... Whatever increases the power of a tribe, either in number or in vigour, gives it an advantage in war; so that other things being equal, societies characterized by sexual relations which are least irregular, will be the most likely to conquer.

Thus the pattern of marriage rule in a society reflects the pressures of social selection under conditions of conflict with other societies. By providing for (a) the systematic replacement of offspring, (b) the political control of individuals, (c) the worshiping of ancestors (and eventually gods), and (d) the sense of loyalty and cohesion that come from strong blood ties, a society is better able to prevail in conflict with others.[19]

Invoking this selection dynamic, Spencer then posited a questionable evolutionary sequence: Early promiscuity was replaced by monogamy which, in turn, was supplemented by polyandry (where the wife can have multiple husbands). Polyandry then lost out to polygyny (where the husband can have multiple wives), which offered greater selective advantage under conditions of conflict. And finally, polygamous marriages, in general, were replaced by a return to the monogamous pattern as rates of conflict among societies decrease. The evolutionary sequence is less interesting than the reasoning as to why systems of multiple marriage (and the corresponding system of descent) emerge as societies grow and why the polygynous system (and the accompanying patrilineal descent system) has selective advantages over polyandry (and presumably the accompanying matrilineal descent system).

Polyandry allows for larger family units that can provide a stable environment for the raising of children and, at the same time, create bonds that further political and social cohesion. But polygyny is an even superior system because it promotes "patriarchy" (read as partrilineal descent), and thus better political organization of chiefs and warriors. It also allows for the rapid replacement of male warriors because some males will have multiple wives to produce larger quantities of new offspring. Moreover, when males stay together in a

17. Ibid., p. 650.
18. Ibid., p. 652.
19. Again, note how conflict and war are the key independent variables in Spencer's analysis.

village, bring wives into their village, have clear knowledge of who
fathered what child (in polyandry, Spencer argued, such cannot be
the case), then there is a much stronger bond between fathers and
offspring, and equally important, this bond can be traced across
generations, creating a system of descent (Spencer seemed unaware
of how this can also be done for matrilineal descent). With a descent
system, ancestor worship and a sense of sacred continuity with the
past are possible, further promoting social integration. And so,
polygynous societies (partilineal descent) will tend to be "more fit"
than societies organized by polyandry (matrilineal descent) under conditions of conflict with other societies.

As the level of war decreases and as alternatives to organizing
human activity increase (i.e., bureaucracies, factories, and other non-
kin groups), monogamy increases. Spencer once again failed to understand descent systems, presumably because the data available to him
in the late 1860s and early 1870s were inadequate. For he assumed
that monogamy is accompanied by a descent system as elaborate
as the unilineal system associated with polygyny (i.e., patrilineal descent). And thus he argues that two sides of the family—the males
and females—are now linked by extensive ties of kinship (when in
fact bilateral systems tend to be truncated, not reckoning descent
to a great degree);[20] and as a result social integration is furthered.

Thus Spencer's analysis of kinship evolution is frequently wrong
in its substantive conclusions. Yet, the mode of analysis remains
interesting: to speculate on how selective pressures in the environment
operated to favor one pattern of kinship over another. For however
flawed, the effort is always to discover the reasons for variations in
the structure of kinship.

Variations in Kinship Structures. For Spencer, the degree of political
centralization to pursue conflict is the critical variable explaining the
structure of kinship. In systems geared to war, males will be involved
in fighting, whereas females will be viewed as property, as productive
labor in the males' absence, and as reproductive vessels who can
replace dead warriors. Under these conditions, polygyny and patriarchy are likely (as is patrilineal descent). Conversely, as a system exists
in relative peace, it will decentralize politically, with the result that
monogamy becomes more likely. For in systems that do not pursue

20. Primarily because bilateral descent can create, not reduce as Spencer hypothesized,
conflict among descent lines.

conflict, males will not need to be replenished at higher rates than females; there will be more emphasis on increased productivity, with males assuming many of the hard labor tasks; and there will be an increase in the equality between the sexes. As Spencer argued:[21]

> The least entangled evidence is that which most distinctly presents this conclusion to us. Remembering that nearly all simple societies, having chronic feuds with their neighbours, are militant in their activities, and that their women are extremely degraded in position, the fact that in the exceptional simple societies which are peaceful and industrial, there is an elevation of women (with) neither race, nor creed, nor culture being in these cases an assignable cause.

CONCLUSION

For its time (1876), Spencer's analysis of "domestic institutions" is insightful, but like that of Marx, Durkheim, and others on kinship it is riddled with mistakes. Yet, Spencer's is probably the best of these early analyses of kinship. In closing, I offer a number of the more useful generalizations that can be extracted from Spencer's overview of kinship processes:

(1) In the absence of alternative ways of organizing societal activities, kinship will become the major organizing principle in a society.

(2) The greater the size of a society without alternative ways to orgainize societal activity, the more elaborate the structure of kinship and the more it will reveal explicit rules of endogamy/exogamy, marriage, and descent.

(3) All other things being equal, the greater the conflict, or potential for conflict, the more elaborate the structure of kinship and the more it will reveal explicit rules of exogamy/endogamy, marriage, and descent.

(4) All other things being equal, societies in conflict will reveal a strong tendency to be patriarchial (and patrilineal).

(5) The more patriarchal a kinship system and the more it exists in a state of conflict, the less is the equality between the sexes, and the more likely are women to be defined and treated as property.

21. Spencer, *Principles of Sociology,* p. 743.

8

The Micro Basis of Society

Spencer on Ceremony

THE PRE- AND SUBINSTITUTIONAL[1]

After discussing the emergence of the first human institution, kinship, Spencer next turned to what he termed "ceremonial institutions." By ceremony, Spencer denoted a broad range of phenomena, but they converge on a concern with the way human interaction proceeds in terms of rituals and symbols. Spencer saw ceremonies as "preinstitutional" in that other institutional structures evolve out of primordial ceremonial practices. The seeds of other institutions, particularly government and religion, are found in the basic ceremonial activities of early humans. Indeed, it is in the stylized interactions, rituals, badges, forms of address, and other ceremonial actions that regulation and control of people in simple societies is achieved.[2] And even as distinctive control structures emerge, such as government and religion, they are constrained by past ceremonial practices. For

within a community, acts of relatively stringent control coming from ruling agencies, civil and religious, begin with and are qualified by,

1. Chapter 1 of Part IV in Herbert Spencer, *Principles of Sociology,* Volume II (New York: Appleton. This part was originally written in 1879), pp. 3-36.
2. Ibid., p. 4.

this ceremonial control; which not only initiates but, in a sense, envelops all other. Functionaries, ecclesiastical and political, coercive as their proceedings may be, conform them in large measure to the requirements of courtesy.[3]

In a real sense, then, ceremony is a subinstitutional process of a society. It is the basic way in which regulation and control is achieved at the interpersonal, micro level. For this "species of control establishes itself anew with every fresh relation among individuals. Even between intimates (ceremonies) signifying continuance of respect, begin each renewal of intercourse."[4]

To emphasize this point, Spencer asserted that social analysts too often examine only the conspicuous macro order and, in the process, overlook the underlying process of ceremonial control.

A chief reason why little attention has been paid to phenomena of this class, all pervading and conspicuous though they are, is that while to most social functions there correspond structures too large to be overlooked, functions which make up ceremonial control have correlative structures so small as to seem of no significance.[5]

Yet, even though ceremonial control is the interactive basis of the macro institutional order, Spencer argued that as political, religious, and economic structures develop, there is a corresponding "decay" and "reduction" of ceremonial control.[6] And therein, he felt, resides one of the basic problems of large, complex societies.

After these initial comments, Spencer then launched into a detailed analysis of various "components of ceremonial rule." I will briefly summarize his review of these components in the next section, with an eye to the more important generalizations that can be culled from his descriptive account.

COMPONENTS OF CEREMONY

Trophies.[7] For Spencer, a "trophy" is an object that symbolizes an activity and achievement. In so doing, it gives "a vague kind of governing power" to its holder.[8] Virtually any object can serve as a trophy, as long as the community of individuals accepts it as

3. Ibid., p. 5.
4. Ibid.
5. Ibid., p. 25.
6. Ibid., pp. 25, 32, 37.
7. Chapter 2 of Part IV in Spencer, op. cit.
8. Ibid., p. 36.

a sign of a particular achievement. Trophies are designed primarily to mark inequality between those who have achieved and those who have not. As such, they establish the other ceremonial practices that are to ensue in an interaction. Thus trophies will be most prominent in "militant" societies where inequality and political authority are prominent features of the social order. Conversely, they will decline in significance as a more "industrial" structure, emphasizing equality and individual freedom, comes to dominate.[9]

Mutilations.[10] In some societies, parts of the body are altered in ways to signify one's position and, thereby, to guide the way in which others respond. Such mutilations can be severe, as is the case with dismembering figures or altering skeletal development, or they can be less physically injurious as is the case with the shaving of hair or the marking of the body with dyes and scar tissue. Mutilations are very much like trophies in that they mark patterns of superordination and subordination.[11] In militant systems, where concern with hierarchy is paramount, mutilations will be most prominent, whereas in industrial systems, they will decrease.[12]

Presents.[13] In a vein similar to the subsequent work of Marcel Mauss,[14] Spencer saw the basic consequence of gift giving as the promotion of social solidarity.[15] The actual value of the gift is far less critical than the fact that it symbolizes and reinforces a social relationship. In militant systems, gift giving can be compulsory as subordinate elites are required to give their more subordinate political leaders presents in order to symbolize their loyalty. Or, in more industrial systems, gifts express a wish to interact or to promote the sentiments underlying the relationship. And so, as industrial forms of society come to dominate, gift giving becomes less compulsory, and the extrinsic value of the gift less critical than its purely symbolic value.[16] But whether freely given or compulsory, a present always creates a reciprocal obligation for the one who receives it. For a

9. Ibid., pp. 49-51.
10. Chapter 3 of Part V, Spencer, op. cit.
11. Ibid., pp. 56-58.
12. Ibid., pp. 78-80.
13. Chapter 4 of Part IV, Spencer, op. cit.
14. Marcel Mauss, *The Gift* (New York: Free Press, 1954, originally published in 1925).
15. Spencer, *Principles of Sociology,* p. 83.
16. Ibid., p. 84.

gift not only symbolizes a relationship, it obligates people to reciprocate in some way, thereby controlling and regulating the relationship.[17]

In gift-giving ceremonies, Spencer felt that he could trace the origins of certain fundamental processes that typify complex societies. In compulsory gifts to superordinate political leaders and religious elites are the primordial ceremonial roots of taxation and ritualized payments to the church. In the obligations to reciprocate the receipt of these gifts can be found, Spencer argued, the source of salaries for those who provide services to elites. Whatever the merits of such arguments, I should emphasize that, unlike our stereotype of Spencer as the quiescent utilitarian, note that his view of taxes, rituals, and salaries is decidedly nonutilitarian. It focuses on how these modern practices have as their underlying basis the present-giving process, which is fundamentally symbolic. Indeed, Spencer argued that taxes, salaries, and ritualized payments to the church still symbolize a fundamental inequality, for each act involves the giving of a present (labor and/or money) by a subordinate in the anticipation of the superordinate reciprocating with services, salvation, money, and other things that the powerful can bestow. The willingness to engage in this process, Spencer asserted, is the result of people's conditioning into more general patterns of gift giving.[18]

Visits.[19] To visit someone is often a mark of homage, or at the very least, a sign that one wants to pursue and preserve a relationship. In systems marked by political centralization, visits are often compulsory, as when a subordinate leader visits a king to affirm loyalty.[20] Similarly, visits to sacred religious temples affirm one's commitment to the hierarchy of supernatural forces.[21] But as the degree of militancy (political centralization and ecclesiastical hierarchies) decreases, then visiting becomes more purely social, but it does symbolize a commitment to a relationship, and in doing, it promotes social solidarity.

Obeisances.[22] The giving of respect and deference, Spencer argued, usually signals a power relationship.[23] Interaction between those with and without power will inevitably involve giving gestures and engaging

17. Ibid., p. 100.
18. Ibid., p. 101.
19. Chapter 5 of Part IV, Spencer, *Principles of Sociology*.
20. Ibid., p. 109.
21. Ibid., p. 113.
22. Chapter 6 of Part IV, Spencer, *Principles of Sociology*.
23. Ibid., p. 126.

in ceremonial activities that signify one's inferiority and another's superiority. The origins of this deference demeanor are found, Spencer contended, in early political and religious hierarchies where subjects had to prostrate themselves before the headman and the priest. As militarism declines, however, deference often occurs among equals as a way to symbolize one's readiness to interact and to promote social solidarity.[24] Thus, in industrial systems where exchange and interaction are less compulsory, obeisances serve the same function of promoting social solidarity, but a solidarity among peers and relative equals.

Forms of Address.[25] The way in which people address each other symbolizes, Spencer argued, the nature of their relationship. Ultimately, forms of address are related to differences in the relative power of individuals.[26] Formal address, coupled with honorific proclamations, signals a power differential, whereas informal address signals just the opposite.[27] And the greater the power differences, the more exaggerated are the forms of address. Yet, with industrial patterns of social organization, formal address can be used to maintain social distance among relative equals,[28] and so, as societies reveal less hierarchy, the old forms of address can still be seen to serve new functions.

Titles.[29] Much like forms of address, titles mark power differentials.[30] They become a way to distinguish superordinates from subordinates, as well as gradations among the ranks. Titles emerge in the initial political and religious hierarchies; and they are greatly accentuated in militant systems where political control and maintenance of social hierarchies are critical. With industrialism, as political decentralization occurs and as hierarchies are replaced by markets and other modes of coordination, the use of titles decreases. Yet, they are still used within organizations where hierarchy is evident; and this continued usage is possible because of the primordial association of titles with political and ecclesiastical hierarchies.[31]

24. Ibid., p. 137.
25. Chapter 7 of Part IV, Spencer, *Principles of Sociology.*
26. Ibid., p. 145.
27. Ibid., p. 156.
28. Ibid., p. 147.
29. Chapter 8 of Part IV, Spencer, *Principles of Sociology.*
30. Ibid., p. 169.
31. Ibid., pp. 177-178.

Badges and Costumes.[32] Spencer saw badges and costumes as a combination of trophies and titles, because they mark distinctions of rank as well as honors and accomplishments.[33] But they are inherently inflationary because they can be copied and emulated by those of lower rank, thereby decreasing their value.[34] And so, they come to be used as much for the marking of membership groups from each other as for rank. Moreover, they became a way to control and regulate the actions of members *within* a group, because in forcing conformity of costumes and badges, they become symbolic signals of people's subordination to the group. However, as militarism decreases, and industrial forms of organization gain dominance, these group demarcation functions increase and their use as markers of rank between unequals decreases.[35]

Fashion.[36] Spencer felt that fashion can potentially mark distinctions of wealth and power; but even more than is the case with badges and costumes, fashion can be emulated.[37] And so, fashion can be a way to decrease outwardly visible signs of inequality. With industrialism, such is very likely to be the case as the wide dissemination of fashion symbolizes decreases in rank and hierarchy, allowing for individual expression. Yet, fashion is an important means of social control because as people conform to the dictates of fashion, they subordinate themselves to a collective force.[38] In so doing, they conform in ways that promote social solidarity.

CONCLUSIONS

Although Spencer is correctly perceived as a macro theorist, he was concerned with the more micro processes of interaction that sustain the institutional order. Indeed, he assumed that the origins of key macro structures could be found in the ceremonial procedures of earlier societies. As with all of his more substantive analyses, the militant-industrial distinction is the critical explanatory variable in understanding ceremonial processes. War and conflict produce political cen-

---

32. Chapter 9 of Part IV, Spencer, *Principles of Sociology.*
33. Ibid., p. 187.
34. Ibid., p. 192.
35. Ibid., p. 197.
36. Chapter 10 of Part IV, Spencer, *Principles of Sociology.*
37. Ibid., p. 210.
38. Ibid., p. 215.

tralization, social hierarchies, and inequalities that in turn, generate a compulsory emphasis upon trophies, mutilations, presents, visits, obeisances, forms of address, titles, badges, and costumes in order to sustain the system of ranks. With political decentralization and lessened concern with rank and hierarchy, however, ceremonial activities decrease. For

> in proportion as the system of exchanging services under contract spreads, and the rendering of services under compulsion diminishes, men dread one another less; and consequently, become less scrupulous in fulfilling propitiatory forms.[39]

What, then, can we conclude from Spencer's analysis? I think that there are a number of interesting generalizations in Spencer's discussion of ceremony; and I have abstracted a list below.[40]

(1) The greater the level of political centralization in a system is, the greater is the level of inequality and the greater is the concern for ceremonial activities demarking ranks.

(2) The greater the concern over ceremonial activities demarking ranks in a system of inequality is, (a) the more likely are people in different ranks to reveal distinctive objects and titles to mark their respective ranks, and (b) the more are interactions among people in different ranks to be ritualized by standardized forms of address and stereotypical patterns of deference and demeanor.

(3) The less the level of political centralization is, the less is the level of inequality; and therefore, the less is the concern with ceremonial activities demarking ranks and regulating interaction among people in different ranks.

As is evident from these generalizations, Spencer saw political institutions and class systems as interrelated in their effects on ceremony.[41] It is not surprising, therefore, that he then turned to an analysis of political institutions and inequality in the next section of *Principles of Sociology.*

---

39. Ibid., p. 223.

40. The reader should note the similarity of these ideas to more modern thinkers, such as *Randall Collins, Conflict Society* (New York: Academic Press, 1975).

41. Indeed, Chapter 9 of Part IV, Spencer, *Principles of Sociology,* is devoted to a "further discussion of class distinctions."

9

Power and Class

Spencer on Political Institutions

Contrary to the popular image of Spencer as an unqualified advocate of laissez-faire stands his emphasis on political processes. For his sociology is permeated with the analysis of how power becomes consolidated and centralized in social systems. Part V of *Principles of Sociology* draws together in 1882 a number of essays that he had published earlier in a variety of periodicals.[1] In this collection of chapters on "political institutions," Spencer developed not only a set of generalizations about political processes in human societies, but also a perspective for analyzing social class structures.

Spencer's work on these topics is often ignored because it is temporally sandwiched between Karl Marx's and Max Weber's work on this topic; and along with sociology's general revulsion against Spencer, it was easily lost. But our ignorance of Spencer's analysis should not be taken as an indicator of its inferior quality next to Marx's and Weber's ideas. Indeed, I think that a fair reading of Spencer will reveal the quality of his political sociology. It is, I believe, as insightful as either Marx's or Weber's work; and in many ways, it provides a corrective supplement to gaps in their work.

1. Herbert Spencer, *Principles of Sociology,* Volume II, (New York: Appleton, 1898). In this reprint edition, Part V appears on pp. 229-643 of Volume II.

THE ELEMENTS OF SPENCER'S
POLITICAL SOCIOLOGY

For Spencer, government emerges because the organization of people into a society creates collective ends and goals that cannot be
met through the exchanges among individuals pursuing private ends,[2]
for "political organization is to be understood as that part of social
organization which constantly carries on directive and restraining
functions for public ends."[3] The most critical "public end" is conflict
with other societies, because political structures first emerged and
have, over the long course of history, been elaborated in response
to conflict. And although war has created many atrocities, it has
stimulated the consolidation of power, which, in turn, has "furthered
the development of social structures."[4]

Although many diverse types of political structures have emerged,
been compounded, and then collapsed, there is a basic tripart form
to all government: (1) a head, (2) a cluster of leaders subordinate
to the head, and (3) a large mass of followers who are subordinate
to both the head and cluster of leaders.[5] From the simplest society
where a head can be observed to the most complex, trebly compound
system (see Figure 6.1), this tripart form is sustained. Moreover,
the "power" behind any political head "existed before governments
arose; governments were themselves produced by it; and it even continues to be that which, disguised more or less completely, works
through them."[6] For Spencer, government must always express public
feelings and sentiments, because rule by coercion alone will create
disintegrative tensions. That is, government must always be legitimated
by ideas that represent the "accumulated and organized sentiment
of the past."[7] Legitimation thus comes from traditional idea systems;
and such systems circumscribe what the head and leadership structure
can do. Indeed, Spencer provided a long list of examples on how
even the most autocratic governments must bend to power of tradition

2. Note how contrary to our popular image of Spencer this position runs.
3. Spencer, *Principles of Sociology*, p. 247.
4. Ibid., p. 231. Spencer was, in fact, quite optimistic about how political structures,
born in war, could now be used for more benign purposes. See Spencer, *Principles
of Sociology*, p. 242.
5. Ibid., p. 243.
6. Ibid., p. 318.
7. Ibid., p. 321.

and public sentiment.[8] And in an oblique critique of Adam Smith's "invisible hand of order" Spencer noted:[9]

> We are familiar with the thought of "the dead hand" as controlling the doings of the living in the uses made of property; but the effect of "the dead hand" in ordering life at large through the established political system is immeasurably greater. That which, from hour to hour in every country, governed despotically or otherwise, produces the obedience making political action possible, is the accumulated and organized sentiment felt towards inherited institutions made sacred by tradition. Hence it is undeniable that, taken in its widest acception (sic), the feeling of community is the sole source of political power: in those communities, at least, which are not under foreign domination.

This last qualification is critical because it signals one of the basic dynamics of the political process: war, conquest, annexation, inadequate basis for legitimation and collapse through internal conflict. For the history of the world's political systems is, to a great extent, a chronology of war, conquest, political consolidation, and then political dissolution. A critical condition encouraging such dissolution is the inability to create the "sacred canopy of tradition" to legitimate the governments of consolidated territories.

In addition to this tension between power and its basis of legitimation, Spencer stressed other inherent sources of change in patterns of political organization. One revolves around the need, on the one hand, to have efficient government staffed by the most qualified, and on the other hand, to have stability of government fostered by the inheritance of leadership.[10] There is a basic tension between these two needs, for one is change-oriented and the other is supportive of the status quo. And each generates its own sources of tension—change and discontinuity versus continuity and rigidity.

Another inherent dilemma of governmental structure is that it is, by its nature, conservative and self-perpetuating. For as government is elaborated, its units become concerned with preserving their power and privilege, and hence, they become conservative. Such conservation generates internal resentment and resistance, often making the society incapable of adapting to change environmental conditions or to external threats.[11]

8. Ibid., p. 326.
9. Ibid., p. 327.
10. Ibid., pp. 260-261.
11. Ibid., p. 256-257.

In this same vein is another problematic feature of political systems. As they grow and perpetuate themselves, they burden a social system with administrative overhead.[12] They are critical to performing large-scale tasks, and yet, they drain a society of its productive resources and personnel. Sustaining a balance between what is critical to meet collective ends and, at the same time, what is essential to sustain economic productivity is always difficult.

Yet another built-in source of tension in the political process revolves around the creation of social classes. Those with power use it to create and sustain privilege, which in turn generates tensions between those with and without resources.[13] Such production of classes is a direct function of the concentration of political power; and so, power creates those class tensions that, under certain conditions, can dissolve existing political institutions.

In sum, there are the overall elements of Spencer's political sociology. Government exists to meet collective ends, initially conflict and defense. It always consists of a tripart division of head, leaders, and followers. It cannot persist without legitimation by ideas tied to the customary practices and traditions of followers. And the very emergence and growth of government creates a number of inherent tensions and dilemmas that inevitably result in its transformation. Such would read a general profile of Spencer's ideas of political processes. But it is in the details of their documentation that these ideas become truly important. And so, in the sections to follow, I will present what by necessity will be a selective analysis of these details.

THE EVOLUTION OF GOVERNMENT

Societies can exist without political structures. Ceremony, kinship ties, and cultural ideas are sufficient to regulate small-scale societies. It is with war that political structures first emerge, because it becomes necessary to have a head, council of war, and followers to carry out the decisions of leaders. And yet, even as political structure emerges "it remains conspicuously subordinate to . . . control of general feeling; both because, while there are no developed governmental structures, the head man has little ability to enforce his will, and because such ability as he has, if unduly exercised, causes desertion."[14]

12. Ibid., p. 250.
13. Ibid., p. 290-310.
14. Ibid., p. 320.

And so, "in its primitive form ... political power is the feeling of the community, acting through an agency which has either informally or formally established."[15]

Those societies that are politically organized to pursue conflict, or to defend themselves, are more likely to survive. Those who are politically organized will tend, Spencer argued, to subjugate those who are not; and thus there is a tendency for politically centralized war-making societies to grow and to spread their institutional patterns. As Spencer noted:[16]

> As, other things equal, groups in which there is little subordination are subjugated by groups in which subordination is greater, there is a tendency to the survival and spread of groups in which the controlling power of the dominant few becomes relatively great.

Political institutions are thus built up in a spiraling process of political organization, war, conquest, annexation of people and territory, political reorganization and elaboration to administer new subjects and territory; then, more war, conquest, annexation, and political elaboration. Yet, "the over-runnings of societies one by another, repeated and re-repeated as they often are, have the effect of obscuring and even obliterating the traces of original structure,"[17] and thus, it is not useful to view political evolution in unilineal terms. Rather, the net effect of war is to create an overall increase in the complexity of the political structure in human societies.

Certain conditions favor the elaboration of political structures through war, conquest, and annexation.[18] One condition is the habitat or nature environment. Can it support a larger population? Does it present barriers to communication, transportation, and interaction? Does it make coercion from a central authority difficult? Another general condition is the degree of similarity between the conquerors and the conquered. Do they reveal similar kinship structures? Do they evidence different religions? Do they have common cultural symbols (language, beliefs, values)? A third condition is the extent of the annexed population's and their conqueror's needs for a common defense against other political aggressors. Are there other hostile

---

15. Ibid., p. 321.
16. Ibid., p. 317.
17. Ibid., p. 317.
18. See Chapter III of Part V, Spencer, *Principles of Sociology,* for the discussion of these.

societies in their environment? Would conquest by those be even more repugnant to an annexed people?

To the extent that these questions are not answered in the affirmative, Spencer argued, dissolution of the politically consolidated system is likely.[19] When coercion must hold the system together, its collapse is inevitable in the long run. And, (a) to the degree that the habitat is inhospitable and difficult logistically, (b) to the extent that the differences between conquerors and their victims remains intact, and (c) to the degree that the need for a common defense does not exist, then political dissolution is accelerated. Conversely, if the habitat is hospitable, if differences are not great or can be reduced through migration, intermarriage, trade, and high rates of interaction, and if outside enemies exist, then political integration of a larger, more populous territory can occur. Such has been the history of political expansion, as societies have consolidated, dissolved, and reconsolidated.

It is in the context of these general processes that Spencer analyzed in more detail the tripart elements of political systems. And so, let me now turn to these.

POLITICAL STRUCTURING AND EVOLUTION

The Rise of Permanent
Political Heads

In the simplest societies, where a political head first emerges, the criterion of "efficiency" or skill at the public task to be performed operates. But "the principle of efficiency, physical or mental, while it tends to produce a temporary differentiation into ruler and ruled, does not suffice to produce a permanent differentiation."[20] For most of human history, such temporary differentiations were typical. But if permanent political structure was to exist, then the criterion of efficiency had to be replaced, to a degree, by the criterion of succession:[21]

> No settled arrangement can arise in a primitive community so long as the function of each unit is determined exclusively by his fitness; since, at his death, the arrangement, in so far as he was a part of it, must be recommenced. Only when his place is forthwith filled by

19. Ibid., p. 277-287.
20. Ibid., p. 341.
21. Ibid., p. 341.

one whose claim is admitted, does there begin a differentiation which survives through successive generations.

In passing, I should note that Spencer argues against elements of the "survival of the fittest" position so often attributed to him. More fundamental than individual conflict and competition within societies is conflict between societies; for it is out of intersocietal conflict that selection pressures for permanent political heads are created.

Such pressures for permanence, Spencer argued, are influenced by the structure of the kinship system. He further hypothesized that "succession through females is less conducive to stable political headships than is succession through males."[22] Again, Spencer was betrayed by his lack of data on descent systems in general, and so, he believed that patrilineal descent and patriarchy create stronger loyalties, more explicit chains of command, and more legitimating connections between a leader and his ancestors who have become deified.[23]

The Growth of the Leadership Structure

Once a permanent differentiation between a permanent leader and followers exists, further elaboration of the political system is possible. Again, war, conquest, annexation, and growing size are the causal forces requiring expansion of the political system. Such expansion occurs through the successive delegation of functions as the complexity and volume of tasks to be performed increases. Such delegation is initially to kindred but eventually it must be to others in different descent lines. The delegation of functions sets into motion a basic dynamic of political organization: To delegate power is, in a real sense, to give power away, and potentially, to create centers of power that can topple a political head. For a king or any political head

is obliged by the multiplicity of his affairs to depute his powers. There follows a reactive restraint due to the political machinery he creates; and this machinery even tends to become too strong for him. Especially where rigorous adhesion to the rule of inheritance brings incapables to the throne.[24]

Thus the criterion of succession and the inevitability of delegation are often at odds and work to produce internal political conflict. Such internal conflict increases as the size of government increases

22. Ibid., pp. 344.
23. Ibid., p. 347-348.
24. Ibid., p. 364.

and is escalated by the process of compounding.[25] For as one ruler
and his armies conquer another, there is always the dilemma of how
to impose rule. If the conquering ruler centralizes the government
and creates a large, hierarchical administrative bureaucracy that fans
out from his position at the top, then power is delegated to functionaries who can use their position to create more power. If, on
the other hand, the ruler simply imposes a more truncated government
on top of the indigenous government of a conquered people, then
the divisions between the conquerors and their victims remain, creating
the potential for further conflict. Spencer listed conditions that
increase or decrease the degree of bureaucratic centralization or
decentralization.[26] If a prolonged war and conquest have been the
basis for the annexation of one society by another, and if military
advisers are prominent in government, then a centralized bureaucracy
is likely. But, if the territories to be governed are vast and pose
geographical obstacles to tight control, if there are large numbers
of people to be ruled, if there is a high degree of diversity and
heterogeneity among the peoples to be governed, then a more
decentralized, "colonial" pattern of compounding is likely.

Along with societal growth, compounding, and the elaboration
of government comes the further differentiation governmental activities
into separate subsystems of government. Spencer emphasized several
of these subsystems, but my summary below will give only a selective
overview of his conclusions.

Military Subsystems.[27] Spencer argued that as humans settled, war
became a constant activity. Initially in the history of warfare, the
general male population could be pulled into the conflict, and thus
a distinctive military subsystem was not evident. However, (a) as
the costs of military activity increase, (b) as the size of the territories
to be militarily controlled increases, and (c) as the differentiation
of a civil bureaucracy increases, then a distinctive military bureaucracy
also emerges and, as a result, the ratio of military to civilian personnel
in a society declines. Once separated, the military subsystem becomes
internally centralized, ideologically unified, and secretive.

Judicial Subsystems.[28] Initially in human history, there was little
differentiation between ruler and judge. But as the volume of adjudica-

25. See Chapter VII of Part V, Spencer, *Principles of Sociology,* pp. 366-395.
26. Ibid., pp. 389-390.
27. See Chapter XII of Part V, Spencer, *Principles of Sociology.*
28. See Chapter XIII of Part V, Spencer, *Principles of Sociology.*

tion in societies increased in response to their increasing size and complexity, then separate judicial functionaries emerged. Such judicial positions come to constitute a distinctive system (1) as the volume of trade, commerce, and contractual obligations increases, (2) as the unfitness of nobles, clerics, and others who have been ascriptively appointed is exposed in the face of growing volume and complexity of adjudication, and (3) as government itself grows, forcing further the delegation of critical tasks. Once created, the judiciary system becomes a self-sustaining bureaucracy that encourages further adjudication by its very existence; and as a result it grows further. And as it grows, it becomes hierarchically organized with its own system of beliefs.

Revenue-Generating Subsystems.[29] As government expands, it must secure money to support itself. War-making dramatically escalates this need for money; and thus government creates mechanisms for usurping the income and wealth of individuals and groups of individuals. Direct taxation of citizens is one mechanism; another is the demands for tribute from subordinate leaders (who tax their followers to secure the tribute); and yet another mechanism is conquest and pillage. There is, Spencer argued, a set of self-reenforcing cycles in war, centralized government, and the creation of taxing formulas. War requires political centralization and such centralization encourages war; war and political centralization generate the need and capacity to tax; the creation of a revenue-generating bureaucracy allows for the regular flow of revenue to support war and a centralized bureaucracy; war-making bureaucracies inevitably grow, forcing further elaboration of the tax-collecting system; and once in place, the tax-collecting subsystem devises ever more efficient (and often abusive) ways to collect taxes.

The Rise of Representative Bodies

At some point in this historical process of compounding expansion of the political system, pressures for representation by the mass of followers mounted. Spencer listed a number of conditions that increase these processes:[30] (1) a lack of war, (2) a decline in strict adherence to religious beliefs, (3) a high degree of geographical dispersion of a population, (4) a large number of hierarchically organized subgroups in a population, (5) a prolonged period of oppression where resentment

---

29. See Chapter XVI of Part V, Spencer, *Principles of Sociology.*
30. See Chapter IX of Part V, Spencer, *Principles of Sociology,* pp. 419-423.

and resistance can build to revolutionary intensity, (6) an increase in the volume of trade and expansion of markets, creating new sources of wealth and power, and (7) an emergence in response to (8) of new beliefs in equality and freedom that, in turn, escalate the sense of deprivation by those subject to repressive political rule.

Spencer felt that conditions (6) and (7) are the most important; and the end result, often after considerable internal conflict and turmoil, is the creation of representative bodies as part of the governmental structure.

Thus for Spencer political evolution is related to societal growth through compounding, typically by virtue of war, conquest, annexation. As societies grow, government also expands and differentiates, creating separate governmental subsystems, and at the same time, centers of counter-power to the political leader or head. As I emphasized earlier, Spencer felt that as political differentiation increases, so do class distinctions. Thus for Spencer, class is not so much a direct reflection of the means and mode of economic production, but of the form and extent of political regulation in a society.

POLITICAL EVOLUTION AND CLASS SYSTEMS

Woven throughout Spencer's discussion of political differentiation is a perspective on social stratification.[31] The earliest differentiations were between males and females; and because males held a monopoly on the implements of hunting, they also controlled the means of coercion.[32] They thus came to dominate females, and in the process, created the first social classes. War with other societies greatly extends stratification in several critical ways. First, it creates the potential for master-slave classes, as the winners of a war often take slaves. Second, it generates divisions between the conquered and conquerors when one population uses war as a way to annex others. Third, war expands government and its elaboration, creating different classes and ranks within the governmental bureaucracy. Fourth, the expansion of government through war allows for the ownership of property by elites, who can use the coercive powers of the government to take the property of other peoples and to maintain their property rights and, hence, their class rank.

31. But see Chapter IX of Part II in particular, Spencer, *Principles of Sociology,* pp. 288-310.

32. Ibid., p. 290.

Once they exist, class divisions tend to perpetuate themselves as long as political centralization exists. Those with power can use this power to gain wealth, which, in turn, can be used to sustain their power and privilege. Such privilege can be passed on from generation to generation; and to the extent that descent groups remain intact, class boundaries can be further sustained by kin solidarity.

Associated with differences in power and wealth come physical differences between members of distinctive classes, as variations in diet, clothing, shelter, and type of labor work to produce people who look and act differently from each other. As Spencer stressed:

> Inequalities of social position, bringing inequalities in the supplies and kinds of food, clothing, and shelter, tend to establish physical differences: to the further advantage of the rulers and disadvantaged of the ruled. And beyond the physical differences, there are produced by the respective habits of life, mental differences, emotional and intellectual, strengthening the general contrast of nature.[33]

And so, these same physical conditions generate different mental outlooks between those in higher and lower classes. Moreover, people who wield power and those who must submit to such power develop varying interpersonal demeanors as well as cultural beliefs that can make individuals in different classes think that existing class divisions are the natural order of things. As Spencer stressed:[34]

> And then there are the respective mental traits produced by daily exercise of power and by daily submission to power. The ideas, and sentiments, and modes of behaviour, perpetually repeated, generate on the one side an inherited fitness for command; and on the other an inherited fitness for obedience; with the result that, in the course of time, there arise on both sides the belief that the established relations of classes are the natural ones.

What, then, breaks patterns of class relations? Spencer's answer is movement from a militant to industrial profile in a society. As individuals can generate wealth through entrepreneurial activities in expanding markets, they accumulate wealth outside the existing political hierarchy and they can use this wealth to change the class system, if only to create a new class for themselves. But as their wealth is based upon individual creative activities, and upon the expansion of open markets, the masses come to believe that they have rights

33. Ibid., p. 309.
34. Ibid., p. 302

as individuals. As a result, they generate pressures to reduce class divisions. Thus, as entrepreneurs generate

> a wealth that is not connected with rank, this initiates a competing power; and at the same time, by establishing the equal positions of citizens before the law in respect of trading transactions, it weakens those divisions which at the outset expressed inequalities of position.[35]

CONCLUSIONS

It is difficult to summarize briefly Spencer's detailed analysis of political institutions. These four hundred pages are filled with propositions and historical illustrations. Only some of the many propositions have been summarized in this chapter. Many more insights are to be found with a firsthand reading of Part V of *Principles of Sociology*. As a way to close this chapter, I have extracted and abstracted a number of key propositions that, I think, are still useful.

Intrasocietal Processes

(1) The degree of stability in government is a positive and additive function of its capacity to balance (a) the needs for efficiency and stable succession, (b) the creation of privileged classes and potential class antagonisms, and (c) the expansion of governmental overhead and nongovernmental productivity.

(2) The degree of political centralization in a society is a positive function of its level and length of conflict with other societies.

(3) The degree of differentiation of subsystems in the government of a society is a positive and additive function of that society's (a) size, (b) volume of internal transactions, and (c) volume of external transactions.

(4) The level of inequality and class formation in a society is a positive function of the degree of centralization of political power.

Intersocietal Processes

(5) The degree of political centralization among a population of societies in a region is a positive function of the overall rate of conflict among these societies.

(6) The degree of political unification among a population of societies in a region that is a positive and additive function of (a) the capacity of one society to coerce others, (b) the degree of structural similarity

35. Ibid., p. 310.

and cultural homogeneity among societies, and (c) the need for a common defense among societies while being a negative and additive function of (d) the size of the territory that a population of societies encompasses and (e) the extent to which barriers in the natural habitat reduce transportation, communication, and migration.

(7) The extent to which political unification among a population of societies reveals a highly centralized, bureaucratic profile is a positive function of the length and intensity of the conflicts that unified them politically.

(8) The extent to which political unification among a population of societies reveals a less centralized and more colonial profile is a positive and additive function of (a) the size of the territory to be governed, (b) the size of the population to be governed, and (c) the level of structural and cultural heterogeneity among the people to be governed.

10

The Elementary and Complex Forms of Religious Life

Spencer on Ecclesiastical Institutions

As I mentioned in an earlier chapter, most of Part I in *Principles of Sociology* is devoted to Spencer's account of primitive religion. In Part VI, written some ten years later,[1] these ideas are woven into a detailed account of religious evolution. In this discussion, Spencer developed a functional argument similar to the one developed by Durkheim over two decades later, but more important is Spencer's analysis of the relationship between political processes and religion. In this short chapter, I will focus selectively on these two themes as I summarize Spencer's overview of religious evolution.

THE FUNCTIONAL AND STRUCTURAL BASIS OF RELIGION

For Spencer, all religions reveal three basic elements.[2] (1) beliefs about supernatural beings and forces, (2) organized groupings of

1. Herbert Spencer, *Principles of Sociology, Volume 3* (New York: Appleton, 1898), Part VI, pp. 3-178. This Part was originally published in 1885.
2. Ibid., p. 6.

individuals who share these beliefs, and (3) explicit activities by individuals directed toward the supernatural forces articulated in religious
beliefs. These elements were among the very first to evolve in human
societies, indicating that they had selective advantage for early societies.
Much of the initial discussion in Spencer's analysis examines the
origin of religion, a topic to which I will return shortly. But the
underlying explanation for the emergence of religion is functional:
religion has always met certain functional needs and thereby promoted
the survival of those populations that developed religion. What are
these needs? It is not until Chapter 9 of Part VI that we begin
to see these needs discussed explicitly,[3] but they are so essential to
his discussion that I will present them at the outset.

In Spencer's view,[4] religious structures promote social integration
through (1) reinforcing cultural values and beliefs by imbuing them
with the power of supernatural forces and (2) strengthening social
structural patterns, especially those revolving around power and inequality, by making them seem to be extensions of the supernatural
will. These functional arguments underlie Spencer's detailed review
of the origins of religion and its subsequent evolution.

THE ORIGINS OF RELIGION

The ultimate origins of religious beliefs, Spencer felt, reside in
human dreams about "another world" of "spirits."[5] It is not a
great jump in the imagination to see this other world as composed
of the "ghosts" of one's relatives and ancestors. Indeed, early humans
probably dreamt of their recently dead relatives and thus concluded
that they were "ghosts" in another realm. Such dreams would, over
time, become codified into beliefs about the powers of ancestors;
and so, the first religions revolved around ancestor worship. Such
worship reinforced the structural basis of traditional societies—that
is, the descent system—and, at the same time, they reinforced the
emerging political leaders of kin groups—giving their leadership continuity with the past and the dead who still existed in a supernatural
world.

The emergence of "gods," Spencer believed,[6] was an extension
of worship toward special and powerful ancestors. If one's run-of-the-
mill ancestors are ghosts, then great individuals become gods whose

3. Ibid., Chapter 9.
4. Ibid., p. 106.
5. Ibid., p. 6.
6. Ibid., Chapter 1.

worship becomes required of both those within and outside the god's kin group. Worship of other than human gods—the sun, for example— are anthropomorphized as super-gods, above and beyond special ancestors, but such beliefs can only build upon the religious base where ancestral gods have already emerged in the religious pantheon. Other objects of worship, such as totems, were at one time simply symbolizations of ancestors or gods, but over time, they emerged as supernatural forces in their own right, disassociated from what they once symbolized.

As social systems gain in complexity, so do religions; and as societies become more hierarchical, so do religions. Religious organization thus reflects the broader social structure of a society. For example, when kinship is the basic organizing principle, ancestor worship is the predominant form of religion; when centralized political power is the prevailing mode of social organization, hierarchical pantheons of gods and lesser supernatural beings are coupled with a hierarchically organized church bureaucracy. For Spencer, then, the origin and subsequent evolution of religion is intimately connected to societal social structure; and it is in tracing this connection that he devoted most of his analysis.

THE EVOLUTION OF RELIGION

The general historical development of religion, Spencer believed, was ancestor worship to ever more complex polytheistic religions, and then, the emergence of monotheism. Such transformations are connected to the political dynamics of a society. For "where the political organization is but little developed, there is but little development of the ecclesiastical organization; while along with a centralized coercive rule there goes a religious rule no less centralized and coercive."[7] The reason for this connection is that religion serves legitimating functions for the political system. Indeed, as the first political heads emerged and then elaborated into chiefdoms, religion legitimated these new powers by linking political leaders to their ancestors who had become deified and whose "blessing" gave the political head the sanction of forces in the supernatural world.[8]

Because political heads first emerged in response to war with other societies, religious evolution is closely connected to the effects of war on political organization. Initial heads could pursue war to the extent that they were legitimated by deified ancestors and by the

7. Ibid., p. 81.
8. Ibid., p. 62.

rituals directed toward the totems of these ancestors. At first, the shaman is both a "medicine man" (who drives away evil ghosts) and "priest" (who makes appeals to the gods).[9] However, as the political structure elaborates in response to external conflict, then these two religious functionaries become clearly differentiated. The "medicine man" role eventually evolves into the profession of medicine and loses many of its religious overtones,[10] whereas the role of priest— that is, those charged with ritual appeals to the gods—becomes elaborated into ecclesiastical bureaucracies that parallel the development of the political bureaucracy.

Spencer felt that the initial differentiation of the priest occurs within the kinship system. Patrilineality is particularly conducive to the designation of a male—typically the eldest male in a descent line—to assume the role of priest.[11] Because this male was also a political leader in historical societies, his special contact with ancestors gave his political power the sanction of the supernatural. As the political system elaborated, however, the increasing complexity of administrative tasks necessitated their delegation; and one of the first to be delegated was priestly functions. Such is especially likely when political development has been the result of conquest of new territories that have created a heterogeneous population whose worship of ancestors, gods, forces, and totems differs from those of the dominant kin group.[12] Similarly, migrations of diverse peoples into a territory also created religious heterogeneity and the consequent delegation of religion to priests. The charge of this emerging priestly class was to consolidate religious dogma and to develop rituals that legitimate the right of political rulers to control and regulate extended and more populous territories.

Such processes, Spencer argued,[13] created polytheism. For as political leaders made war and conquered new territories, and as the task of consolidating diverse deities was delegated to the priests, polytheism emerged and the gods and supernatural forces were organized into a coherent pantheon. The inequalities among the gods reflected the patterns of political inequality—conquering people's gods will be high in the hierarchy and those of the conquered will be lesser gods in the hierarchy.[14]

9. Ibid., p. 41.

10. This made much more explicit in Part VII on "professional institutions," Herbert Spencer, *Principles of Sociology*. In fact, most professions—art, music, medicine, architecture, and the like—are seen as having their roots in religion.

11. Ibid., pp. 48-50.

12. Ibid., p. 65.

13. Ibid., p. 71.

14. Ibid., p. 74.

As the complexity of this reconciliation of gods increases with further conquests, the priestly class grows. Its bureaucracy became larger and its land holdings and other sources of wealth increased. The more warlike a society, the more the political system relied upon the ecclesiastical bureaucracy; and the more this bureaucracy was needed to consolidate religious ideas and to legitimate political activities, the greater was the capacity of the ecclesiastical bureaucracy to extract wealth and privilege from political elites. Moreover, the gods of such religions are likely to be ferocious and vengeful, reflecting the violence of war-making societies.[15]

Monotheism arose only when the church bureaucracy was large and when hierarchies of gods had been clearly developed. For once the idea of hierarchy among gods is established, Spencer felt that there was an inevitable trend toward monotheism.[16] For if there is hierarchy, some god must be at the top and the lesser gods increasingly fall out of the pantheon in relation to the powers of the god at the pinnacle of the hierarchy. Moreover, a monotheistic religion made it much easier to legitimate monarchical forms of government, because if rulers can be legitimated by one god, the task of religious sanctioning is greatly facilitated over what exists when a monarch is forced to seek legitimation from a collage of gods in a complex pantheon. Additionally, a monarchical government born from conquest, as well as a privileged church bureaucracy, often created conditions for religious revolutions that tended to be monotheistic, as it is easier to mobilize public passions around one god than a complex pantheon. The result was a series of pressures toward monotheism at that point in history when the church and state bureaucracy had reached an elaborated stage of development.

Yet, despite the symbiotic relationship between church and state, there is always a tension between them.[17] This tension grows as the powers of the church increase. Spencer then listed some of these powers:[18] the claim of religious leaders as the bestowers of legitimation on political elites; the claim of priests as the only conduit to the supernatural realm; the claim of the church and priestly class as a center of culture, knowledge, literacy, art; and the claim of the church on considerable property and wealth. As the church becomes a self-serving and self-perpetuating bureaucracy[19] filled with members of a privileged class of citizens, then conflicts between it and the

15. Ibid., see Chapter V of Part VI.
16. Ibid., see Chapter VII of Part VI, especially p. 75.
17. Ibid., see Chapter VII of Part VI.
18. Ibid., pp. 141-145.
19. Ibid., p. 147.

self-serving political elite are increasingly evident.[20] At various points in history, political leaders thus began to work at reducing the powers of the church and at securing a more civil and secular bases of legitimation—that is, courts, constitutions, and even representative bodies of advisors.

Such trends are accelerated with the expansion of trade and markets as well as with the consequent elaboration of courts, laws, and new economic structures. Moreover, in recent times, as science became a more dominant belief system in an entrepreneurial and mercantile environment, it too challenged religion and reduced its powers. And once the force of tradition is broken, and as economic changes associated with the Industrial Revolution fostered a sense of individual rights,[21] political pressures mounted for a more representative government. The end result was the development of secular sources of legitimation and a corresponding decrease in the powers of the church.

CONCLUSION

Spencer's overview of religion is much more elaborate than my brief summary. More than his other chapters on basic institutional processes, these on religion are descriptive and historical. And so I will not try to pull from them more abstract generalizations. But in closing, I would emphasize several points. First, Spencer's analysis represents a political interpretation of religion. Religion emerges, persists, and elaborates as a function of war, conquest, and empire building. Second, his overview is functional but invokes a social selection mechanism. The evolution of religion has selective advantage for societies that have engaged in war and conquest. Third, Spencer's discussion is "structuralist" in that religion is seen to reflect the social structural arrangements of a society. The nature of the religious pantheon and the organization of priests mirror the more general social structure of a society.

I am not sure just how useful these ideas are for contemporary sociology; for the decade between 1874-1884 when they were developed and first published, they are very insightful and anticipate those of other scholars who are often given credit for these lines of analysis. So, if only to set the record straight, this short review has been necessary.

20. Ibid., p. 130.
21. Ibid., pp. 132-133.

11

Economy and Society

Spencer on Industrial Institutions

The last section of *Principles of Sociology*[1] was published in 1896, some twenty years after he began this extended work. In these chapters, Spencer analyzed "industrial institutions," or economic processes. With this extended discussion of economy and society, Spencer pronounced his synthetic philosophy completed, although he lamented[2] that at his advanced age he could not complete his proposed volume on linguistic, intellectual, moral, and aesthetic processes. More than any of the previous portions in *Principles of Sociology*, these last chapters are the most flawed with evaluative overtones; and yet, as I will emphasize, his critiques of socialism and trade unionism have contemporary relevance. As he admitted, his critiques "should not be included in an account of Industrial Institutions,"[3] but he could not resist commenting upon the two great social movements of his time.

These polemics aside, Spencer's discussion of the economy revolves around an historical description of the transformation in basic elements of the economy. Spencer began with an overview of economic evolu-

1. Herbert Spencer, *Principles of Sociology* (New York: Appleton, 1898, originally published 1896). This last section, Part VIII contains twenty-four chapters, pp. 327-611 of Volume 3.
2. See the preface to Part VIII.
3. Herbert Spencer, *Principles of Sociology*, p. 590.

tion from its simplest beginnings among hunters and gatherers to its most complex industrial forms. As with all discussions of evolution, he stressed the discontinuity and diversity of economic change. For as populations adapted to diverse environments, they experimented with ways of performing economic tasks. Some of these were successful, others were failures; and so, economic "is not linear but divergent and re-divergent."[4] Yet, although the conditions of early environments created resistance to economic change, they also forced the development of new technologies that, in turn, successively decreased the resistance of the environment and, at the same time, encouraged the development of ever new modes of economic organization. Economic evolution is thus exponential, and after a slow start, it accelerates not only because of the "increase of the operative forces, but it exhibits a further acceleration resulting from decrease of resistances."[5]

The key processes in economic evolution, Spencer argued, are the expanded capacity of production and distribution, the accumulation of capital, and the changing mechanisms for organizing labor around the means of production. Each of these topics will guide my presentation in this last chapter on Spencer's sociology.[6]

ECONOMIC PRODUCTION AND DISTRIBUTION

Production

Economic production increases as the gathering of resources and their conversion into commodities revolves around tools and nonhuman sources of power. The motive force behind the development of tools and new sources of power is the escalation of human needs.

> As a means of satisfying the desires, production increases as the desires multiply and become stronger; and the order in which the different kinds of production develop, is determined by the relative strengths of desires.[7]

In passages that are reminiscent of Marx, Spencer argued that as soon as one set of needs is satisfied, new ones arise.

> Of course the primary needs for food and warmth have first to be in some degree met; and of course, the first kinds of production

4. Ibid., p. 331.
5. Ibid., p. 327.
6. This listing is out of Spencer's order of presentation. Also, some topics are omitted or collapsed together.
7. Herbert Spencer, *Principles of Sociology,* p. 364.

are those subserving these primary needs. But long before bodily wants
are fully satisfied mental wants prompt other kinds of production.

As production increases in response to escalating needs, it is inevitably transformed. First, the direct relationship between work
and product is severed as the division of labor forces specialization
of tasks. Second, much production is secondary and tertiary in
the sense of facilitating with services and products the production
of basic consumer goods. Once established, such processes are self-
reinforcing. The effectiveness of a division of labor causes its further
development; and the increasing volume of primary production
necessitates even more secondary and tertiary forms of production.[8]
And as overall production of goods and services increases, so must
the process of distribution.

These self-reinforcing processes that expand production can ac-
celerate only if a society avoids war, because Spencer believed that
wartime production and the centralization of power retard broadly
based economic growth. Historically, as long as war consumed a
society, economic productivity could not increase; and thus for great
periods of human history, economic stagnation and retrogression
typified the warring societies of the world. For the

> progress of industrial activity is thus in several ways dependent on
> the decline of militant activity. While war increases the mortality of
> men, it decreases by overwork the fertility of women and so checks
> population; it here abstracts and thereby destroys the surplus produce
> or capital which industry has accumulated; and it breeds contempt
> for peaceful occupations and hence leaves them without good guidance.[9]

Conversely, peace increases population size, requiring an escalation
of productivity. It also allows people's wants, needs, and desires
to expand, creating demand for new products. And it allows for
the accumulation of capital for production, and it prompts the
development of new, nonmilitary technologies.[10]

For Spencer, then, productivity is a negative function of external
conflict and political centralization. Only when a society is not
consumed with war can escalating wants and needs lead to the
formation of capital, the development of new technologies, and
the expansion of the productive process through the division of
labor necessary to meet these needs. War distorts production to
military purposes, depletes capital, suppresses wants and needs for

8. Ibid., p. 371.
9. Ibid., pp. 367-368.
10. Ibid., p. 368.

consumer goods, and encourages the development of only military technologies.

Distribution

Spencer's analysis of distribution is more extensive than his treatment of production. As production increases there is more to distribute, and thus distribution processes become more elaborate. But more important, "distribution is a necessary concomitant of the division of labor"[11] because as corporate units and individuals perform specialized functions, "there must evolve a system of transference from one to another of their respective products."[12]

Spencer saw the history of distribution as tied to the elaboration of exchange processes. Exchange is rooted in basic ceremonial processes among the first human societies. For "the very idea of exchange, without which there cannot begin commercial intercourse and industry, has itself to grow out of certain ceremonial actions."[13] Such actions reinforce underlying sentiments and beliefs, and thus exchange always has deep noncontractual roots. The first exchanges involved simple barter, but as Spencer emphasized, there are always problems of assessing the respective value of the objects in barter. As a result, exchange is limited, and hence, so is the process of economic distribution.

Historically, these limitations created pressures for developing measures of equivalence among objects. For only when a society had a currency that allows objects as well as labor to be quantitatively specified could the process of exchange and distribution expand significantly. Spencer argued that the first currencies were objects that all people wanted and that could be divided into approximately equal units. Such objects as food, skins, weapons, and ornaments were probably the first currencies because they were valued and because the value of other objects could be expressed in terms of them.[14]

It is from decorative ornaments and jewelry as a currency, Spencer believed, that the first coins emerged. Ornaments and jewelry usually contained precious metals and the amount of such metal could be determined (by either size or weight) and used as a measure of value. Coins of these precious metals simply became a more precise way to express value; and because they could be used to pay for any object or labor, the rate as well as the volume of

11. Ibid., p. 373.
12. Ibid.
13. Ibid., p. 388.
14. Ibid., p. 394.

exchange and distribution could increase.[15] But coins are bulky, and so, paper money was invented to further the process of exchange. Yet, paper money is easily inflated because, unlike precious metals, political regimes can easily issue more of it, and as a consequence, deflate its value. Still the invention of paper money greatly increased the capacity for distribution in a society, for by

> making exchange more facile, a trustworthy currency enormously extended and eased the process of distribution. The means of making most purchases could now be carried about on the person. Definite estimations of values of things bought and sold, could be made—*prices* arose. The amounts payable for labour of various kinds could be currently known. And, above all, the obstacles to distribution which had resulted from inability to find those who personally needed goods to be disposed of, entirely disappeared. Moreover, with the establishment of prices and current knowledge of them, transactions between buyer and seller lost, in large measure, the arbitrary character they previously had. Lastly, as a concomitant effect, arose the possibility of competition. Prices could be compared, and the most advantageous purchases made; whence, along with advantage to the buyer, came checks and stimuli to the distributor.[16]

Thus money increases distribution which, in turn, encourages more production. Price competition increases the efficiency of production, stimulating a search for new ways to produce goods more cheaply. Yet a money currency imposes certain limitations. It requires immediate payment; and so, over time, credit-paper was invented to allow those with property and assets to pay for goods and services without actually possessing the currency in hand. Once the concept of credit was institutionalized, then the structural base of all contemporary exchange systems—banks, clearing houses, and financial markets—was laid.

CAPITAL FORMATION

The expansion of production requires investments of capital. Without money it is not possible to accumulate productive capital in great quantities. For as long as resources were in commodities, they could not be used in flexible ways to buy machines, energy, labor, and raw materials to produce varieties of goods. Thus the evolution of money allowed for more flexible patterns of capital formation.

15. Ibid., p. 399.
16. Ibid., pp. 400-401.

One of the first ways to use money in order to create capital is to pool it. The joint stock company is simply an outgrowth of earlier trading associations and partnerships, for as the number of individuals in a population whose assets can be converted to money increases, a much larger pool of capital is potentially available for investment in production.[17] Without such pooling, large-scale economic productive tasks cannot be performed, because no one individual has sufficient wealth. For who, Spencer asked, would have the resources to perform industrial production on a mass scale. Government is the only other potential economic actor with sufficient resources to undertake large-scale industrial production, but if its "execution had been left to the Government, conservatism and officialism would have raised immense hindrances."[18] And so, the joint stock company and eventually the creation of new markets in stocks and bonds emerged, facilitating the pooling of capital necessary for production revolving around machines driven by inanimate energy and attended by masses of labor. And once such a mechanism for pooling capital exists, both the volume and diversity of goods that can be produced is dramatically increased.

THE ORGANIZATION OF LABOR

Spencer devoted the bulk of Part VIII on the economy to an historical overview of the varying patterns in the organization of labor.[19] He began with kinship as the organizing principle, and then, he successively discussed communities, guilds, slavery, serfdom, contracted labor, trade unionism, and socialism as organizing processes. In this overview, which—I should stress—is filled with historical and ethnographic detail, Spencer developed some interesting generalizations and made a number of prophetic observations about trade unionism and socialism. In my brief summary, I will highlight these generalizations and observations, leaving Spencer's empirical documentation of his assertions to the interested reader.

Kinship Regulation of Labor

Early regulation of labor, Spencer observed, occurred within a kinship system. And, as political and ecclesiastical processes are

17. Ibid., p. 530.
18. Ibid., p. 532.
19. Ibid., p. 412.

also merged within kinship in the simplest societies, economic activity is intimately connected to politics and religion. The long-term historical trend, however, has been for the regulation of labor to become increasingly free of politics and religion, although Spencer felt that modern socialism represents a return to older forms of aristocratic political domination.

Within kinship, regulation is determined by sex and age as well as by the authority inhering in the descent system. Indeed, a descent rule, especially a patrilineal rule, creates an organizational hierarchy that organizes the division of labor much like a modern bureaucracy.[20] Control in this hierarchy is facilitated by ancestor worship, where the dead still influence the present and the living, and by the passing of property through the male line, where material incentives can keep labor in line.

As kinship systems grow into "large classes" (Spencer did not have the concept of moieties available to him), then kinship and community structures overlap. A given kin group is likely to control a community or cluster of communities. Thus, as communal forms of regulating labor emerge, they do so from a population of residence held together by blood ties.

Communal Regulation of Labor

Early communities were coextensive with kinship units, but as they grew through war and conquest, "outsiders" (slaves, migrants, refugees, etc.) were added to the kinship base. Such outsiders came under the control of extended household units and were thereby regulated. Assignments of land, economic tasks, and other activities were typically made by the heads of these extended families. But as communities grow, the capacity of kinship to regulate labor decreases.[21] And it is from the regulatory problems of organizing labor in larger communities that alternatives to kinship control began to emerge. One of the first alternatives is guild regulation of labor.

Guild Regulation of Labor

Spencer felt that guilds evolved from family groupings that had specialized in certain economic tasks within a growing community.[22] As communities grew, however, guilds often added outsiders to the clusters of relatives. But both kin and non-kin were highly restricted

20. Ibid., p. 431.
21. Ibid., p. 447.
22. Ibid., p. 449.

in their activities, because the goal of a guild is to maintain a monopoly on certain specialized activities. Moreover, the guilds would create agreements among themselves to assure that each could maintain its viability against potential competition. Additionally, guilds often developed taxing powers over their members, thereby increasing their control.

But Spencer believed that guilds created the very condition for their own destruction. By maintaining such control over their members' activities in urban areas, they generated resentments among those who wanted more freedom. And so, many skilled workers fled urban communities to the rural areas where they could use their skills more freely. As they did so, they could undercut the guilds by producing new and better products and by providing better services than the guilds.

Slave Regulation of Labor

In all types of societies, Spencer asserted that slavery has been practiced. The first descent grouping often took slaves as they fought their neighbors and other kin groups. And thus alongside other forms of labor regulation is the regulation of slaves. Spencer thus saw the origins of slavery as residing in war. When males are being killed or are away, their labor needs to be replaced; and it is often convenient to enslave one's enemies, especially children who can be socialized into a slave role.

Spencer distinguished between undeveloped and developed slavery. In undeveloped slavery, the number of slaves is small and each is typically incorporated into a kin group as a kind of "special servant." In developed slavery, there is a mass of slaves who constitute a distinctive social class. When a slave class exists, the stratification system tends to become divided into a tripart form of military class, free industrial class, and slave class.

Slavery cannot, Spencer argued, endure in competition with free labor. For the "relative lack of energy, the entire lack of interest, the unintelligent performance of work, and the greater cost of supervision, make the slave an unprofitable productive agent." And so, as the pool of free labor grows, slavery "tends gradually to disappear."[23]

Feudal Regulation of Labor

Like slavery, feudalism was the product of war in historical societies. As one population conquered another, there was always the problem of regulation and administration of new territories. Or, as populations

23. Ibid., p. 478.

sought to defend themselves from invaders, local communities subjugated themselves to those political leaders that could protect them. Thus, whether for defense or as a result of conquest, war produces feudalism in technologically less advanced societies. Because war has been so frequent historically, feudalism has been a pervasive form of social organization.[24] In the process of creating a feudal system, there emerges a corresponding system for organizing labor, serfdom. In return for protection and for capital (land, implements, seeds, and the like), serfs agreed to be taxed, to perform economic tasks, and to support the political activities of their feudal lord.

Such a system was particularly viable, Spencer felt, as long as war persisted and serfs felt vulnerable. But as war decreased, and the level of threat declined, the subjugation of the serf to the powers of lord created internal tensions. Serfs will come to resent taxation of their surplus; they will become angered over their inability to accumulate their own capital; and they will increasingly be resentful of their lack of freedom. Moreover, because the feudal system involved compulsive labor, it was inherently inefficient; and as other societies moved out of feudalism, those that remained were vulnerable to invasion and conquest.[25]

The Emergence of Free Labor

The compulsory organization of labor, Spencer believed, created pressures for free labor and contract. For example, serfdom generates resentments; guild members leave to rural areas in search of more freedom; and slaves seek to purchase their freedom.[26] Spencer argued that the ceremonial roots of freely entered labor contracts can be found in gift ceremonies where the receipt of a gift imposes an obligation to reciprocate. And thus, as traditional modes of labor regulation declined, there was already in place a subinstitutional basis for free labor. As free labor sought to contract its services, pressures for currency and writing increased, as there needed to be a more precise way to establish the rate of exchange for work performed and remuneration received.[27]

Free labor was both a cause and consequence of new modes of economic productivity in which inanimate energy was coupled with machines and workers in a factory system. Such a system needs workers who are free to sell their labor, and at the same time, it

24. Ibid., p. 479.
25. Ibid., p. 491.
26. Ibid., pp. 493-505.
27. Ibid., pp. 510-514.

creates a pool of free labor by destroying traditional mechanisms for regulating labor. Spencer saw the factory system as a form of organization that "parallels in its divisions military organization."[28] It creates a rigid hierarchy for organizing work, and in so doing, it creates problems for workers.

For in increasing productivity, and in helping to generate a wide variety of consumer goods that can be enjoyed by workers, the factory system forces workers to lose their role as active producers.[29] In long passages that are reminiscent of Marx, Spencer lamented[30] the "continually decreasing sphere of human agency"; he decried the "monotony" that "taxes the nervous system"; he was repulsed by the physical harm of "breathing vitiated air"; he recognized that labor is not really free because to leave one job and take another is "little more than the ability to exchange one slavery for another"; and he pessimistically concluded that "the coercion of industrial workers" is little different than former forms of bondage.

Trade Unionism

The consequence of this degraded situation among workers is to generate awareness of their interests in raising wages, in shortening work hours, and in improving working conditions.[31] Yet, despite Spencer's sympathetic portrayal of the plight of workers, he was clearly against trade unionism. He saw it as creating several problems.

First, it creates a wage-price spiral, because increased wage costs for produces are passed on in the form of higher prices; and so "each trade unionist, while so much the more in pocket by advanced wages, is so much the more out of pocket by having to buy things at advanced rates."[32] Second, industrial strikes cost the workers more than they gain, because what they lose in wages and what debts they must incur during a strike are rarely made up by increased wages, especially when they lead to a general increase in prices.[33]

Third, excessive wage demands will drive some companies to the point where they cannot make a profit and must shut down, thereby eliminating the jobs of workers. Fourth, excessive wage demands also drive capital away to pools of lower-priced workers; and so,

28. Ibid., p. 516.
29. Ibid., p. 523.
30. Ibid., pp. 522-525.
31. Ibid., p. 537.
32. Ibid., p. 546.
33. Ibid., p. 549.

if wages in one nation are too high, companies go overseas in search of cheaper labor, once again eliminating the jobs of workers.[34]

Despite these reservations, Spencer saw unionism as inevitable in light of the working conditions among industrial workers. Yet there is no mistaking Spencer's evaluative tone against labor unions (one of the few places in *Principles of Sociology*, I should emphasize, where Spencer is evaluative). For Spencer saw unionism as moving inevitably into socialism, which, he argued, would create more problems than it resolves.

Socialism

For Spencer, "a state of universal brotherhood is so tempting an imagination, and the existing state of competitive strife so full of miseries, that endeavors to escape from the last and enter into the first are quite natural—inevitable even."[35] But socialism, Spencer believed, presented certain fundamental flaws.

First, socialism assumes that it is possible in large, complex systems to have such ideological consensus and solidarity among members of a population that the connection between merit and rewards can be eliminated. That is, workers will be willing to take in "accordance with their needs" rather than their merits and performances.[36] Such a state of affairs, Spencer argued, is not possible without massive coercion by the government.

Second, socialism assumes an altruism in which individuals will sacrifice their well-being and that of their immediate family in order to subsidize strangers who are less able and productive. Spencer believed that to ask individuals to sacrifice benefits to themselves and their families is not possible without being imposed by the coercive powers of the state.[37]

Third, to subjugate one's personal interests to the community means, in essence, that "individuals are to be possessed by the state; which, while it supports them, is to direct their labors."[38] Spencer saw such a turn of events as retrogression back to more traditional forms of regulating labor, such as serfdom.

Fourth, to regulate labor in the name of the collective, "there is implied a vast and elaborate administrative body";[39] and when

34. Ibid., p. 550.
35. Ibid., p. 557.
36. Ibid., p. 581.
37. Ibid., pp. 582-583.
38. Ibid., p. 587.
39. Ibid.

one asks of the bureaucracy, "how is it to be regulated, there is no such satisfactory answer."[40] And without regulation, there is created "a new aristocracy for the support of which the masses would toil; and which being consolidated, would wield a power far beyond that of any past bureaucracy."[41]

For Spencer, then, the state does not "wither away." Indeed, its hierarchical structure becomes a new basis for stratification and for exploitation of workers. Although there is a heavily evaluative tone in Spencer's critique, I think that there is considerable merit in the argument. We should recall also that he made this argument two decades before the Russian Revolution; and in light of its aftermath, his predictions seem justified.

CONCLUSION

This chapter completes my review of Spencer's sociology. I trust that many of the misconceptions about Spencer's work have been overcome and that contemporary sociologists will be willing to at least read Spencer with the same passion and devotion that they now read other early masters. However, as I have noted many times in other works, sociology's devotion to its masters has reached a point of shackling our theoretical imagination, as we must be careful to cite Marx, Weber, Durkheim, and others. Indeed, at least half of sociological theory is reanalysis of these early masters.

Thus, in encouraging that we take a close look at Herbert Spencer, I am not advocating more history of ideas, more philosophizing, more scholasticism. Rather, I believe that we should look at Spencer because we have not used his ideas to develop theory to the extent that we have employed the ideas of other historical figures. We have spent, indeed wasted, a great deal of time rediscovering Spencerian sociology; it would be more efficient to examine it firsthand and profit from it to the same degree as we have for Marx, Weber, and Durkheim. But in the end, we should leave all of these masters in the background and use our own creative abilities to build theory.

In this last chapter, as well as all of the others on Spencer's institutional analysis, there is much insight. Most of the chapters to Part VIII are descriptive, but they are filled with interesting historical generalizations. These are not theoretical, and so, I will not summarize them as I have periodically done in other chapters. But his observations

40. Ibid., p. 588.
41. Ibid., p. 589.

on the evolution of distribution processes, the varying forms of regulating labor, and on the dilemmas of state socialism are worth a careful reading, because they complement and correctly contradict the analyses of Marx, Weber, and Durkheim. In this final series of chapters, as in all of Spencer's work, there is still much to be learned. I hope that sociology is not too prejudiced to reexamine the works of this great thinker.

Author Index

Abrahamson, M., 12
Anderson, T. R., 72
Andreski, S., 12

Beeghley, L., 22, 51, 73, 93
Blau, P., 71, 74
Brinton, C., 63
Buckley, W., 32

Carneiro, R. L., 12
Comte, A., 16, 17, 18, 28, 50, 54
Coser, C. A., 9, 12

Duncan, D., 96
Durkheim, E., 11, 13-15, 17, 18, 20, 22, 29, 34, 51, 52, 54, 55, 58, 61, 64, 66, 73, 74, 75, 87, 100, 115, 136, 153-154

Freeman, J. H., 72

Garstang, J., 96
Gibbs, J. P., 72
Giddens, A., 63
Goldman, P., 72

Hannan, M. T., 72
Hobbes, T., 50, 56

Kasarda, J. D., 72

Labovitz, S., 72
Lenski, G., 63, 92
Lenski, J., 63
Long, R., 96
Lukes, S., 22

Malinowski, B., 52, 102
Martineau, H., 16, 50
Maryanski, A. R., 14, 17, 59, 62, 103

Montesquieu, C., 68
Marx, K., 11, 13, 15, 34, 87, 115, 123, 143, 151, 153
Mauss, M., 54, 65, 118
Mead, G. H., 15
Miller, J., 72
Miller, J. G., 31, 32
Morgan, J., 87
Murdock, G., 86, 102, 103

Noell, J. J., 72

Pareto, V., 64, 81
Parson, T., 15, 49, 50-52, 59, 60-61, 63, 68, 92
Peel, J.D.Y., 11
Perrin, R. G., 11, 63-64
Plato, 50, 56

Radcliffe-Brown, A. R., 14
Ritzer, G., 30

Scott, R., 73
Scott, W. A., 73
Simmel, G., 84
Stephen, E. G., 72
Sumner, W. G., 107

Torday, E., 96
Tredder, H., 86
Turner, J. H., 47, 51-52, 58, 62, 73, 87, 93, 103
Tyler, E., 87

von Bertalanffy, L., 30

Wallerstein, I., 64
Warner, L., 102
Weber, M., 11, 13, 87, 123, 153-154

Subject Index

Abstract: principles, 73-84; sciences, 27-28; theory, 27
Aggregation, 23, 29, 33, 38, 65, 86
Ancestor Worship, 137-138
Anomie, 75

Badges, 121
Biases, 23; cognitive, 23-24; emotional, 23; mitigation of, 23-30; positional, 23-25; public moods, 24; self interest, 24; sensationalism, 24; temporal, 26; vested interests, 26
Body Social, 50

Capital, 146; economic, 147; effects of war, 144
Causal/Cause, 17; analysis, 28, 61; effects, 28; modeling, 29
Centralization: of government, 124-135; of power, 134-135; of societies, 93-95
Ceremony: components of, 117-121; defined, 116; power-class, 122
Civil Law, 54, 55
Class Systems: bureaucratized, 132; effects of politics on, 133; industrialization and, 133-134; religion and state, 139-141; sexual, 132; slave, 132
Colonial Systems, 130, 135
Complexity, 36-38, 41, 57, 60
Compounding, 86; aggregation, 86; conquest, 87; societal, 87-91
Conflict, 76-77, 79, 82, 107; church and state, 140; class, 132; effects of government on, 124-127; effects of religion on, 138-139; intersocietal, 129
Consciousness, 58
Control, problems of, 70-75

Coordination,, problems of, 21, 75
Costumes, 121
Cybernetics, 30
Cycles, 44, 65

Data: collection, 27; problems in, 25-26
Decentralization: of power, 82; of societies, 93-95
Dedifferentiation, 41
Deductive Theory, 65
Dependency Theory, 64
Derived Factors, 53-54
Descent, 111-114
Descriptive Sociology, 96-98
Destructuring, 33, 44, 64-65
Dialectical, 68; analysis, 79
Differentiation, 21-23, 29, 36-37, 43, 55, 57, 64-66, 73-74; models of, 69-71
Dissimilarity, 76-77
Distributive: axes, 75, 86; functions, 60; needs, 61; processes, 62; problems, 69-71, 78; structures, 22
Distributive System: differentiation of, 78; economy and, 145-146; evolution of, 87-91; society and, 93-95
Division of Labor, 143-144

Ecological Concentration, 74
Economy, elements of, 147-153; evolution of, 142-143; power and, 144; war and, 144
Empiricism, 16
Endogamy, 111-112
Energy, 39-40
Enlightenment, the, 34
Entrepreneurial, 77
Entropy, 30, 33, 38

Equilibrium, 33, 39-40, 44, 64-65
Ethnographic Data, 83. See descriptive sociology
Evolution, 14, 33-38, 55, 65; description of, 109; law of, 34, 38, 41, 65-66; non-lineal, 108; social selection, 107-108; stages of, 87-99
Exchange: ceremonial, 145; evolution of, 145-146
Exogamy, 111-112
External System, 60
External Threat, 19, 76

Factory System, 151
Fashion, 121
Feudalism, 149-150
First Principles, 32-33, 35, 43, 51, 56, 62
Fission, 69, 71
Force, 35, 37-38, 42, 65
Friction, 41
Functions, 17, 55-57
Functional: analysis, 17; needs, 60; requisites, 59
Functionalism, 50, 55; analytical, 58; descriptive, 103-104; explanatory, 103

General Systems, 30-31, 43; Generalizing, 27
Grand Theory, 27
Group Selection, 107
Growth, 21, 29; of populations, 53; systems, 33, 42-43, 64
Guilds, 148-149
Heterogeneity, 36-37, 40, 53, 65-66
Hierarchy of Sciences, 28
Homogeneous, 36-37, 37, 65-66
Human Relations Area Files: Spencer's approach, 95-105; tabular system, 96-97

Ideas, 55, 100
Ideologies, 81, 83
Inequality, 76. See class systems
Industrial Societies, 92-95; as description, 104; as explanation, 105
Information, 30
Inorganic Realm, 52-53
Integration, 23, 29, 38, 41-49, 55-59, 64-68; ceremonial basis, 116-127; problems of, 66-68, 82
Interdependence, 66-68
Institutions: analysis of, 107-109; ceremonial, 116-127; definition of, 106; domestic, 109-115; economic, 142-153; political, 123-135; religious, 136-141
Interests, conflict of, 77
Internal System, 60
Internal Threat, 76

Judicial Systems, 130-131

Kinship, 109-115; among primates, 111; emergence of, 109; evolution of, 111-115; functions of, 110; integration of, 111-112; selection for, 110; variations in, 114-115

Labor: communal, 148; feudal, 149-150; free, 150-151; guild, 148-149; kin-based, 147-148; union, 151
Laissez Faire, 10-13, 79
Laws, 18. See principles
Lawful Regularities, 18-19. See principles
Linnean Classification, 97
Living Systems, 32

Marriage, 113
Mathematics, 19, 20
Matter, 35-37, 65
Meaning, 25
Meaningful Action, 25
Measurement, 22
Mental Discipline, 26-27
Meta Theory, 61
Micro Analysis, 117
Micro Control, 117

Militant Societies, 79, 92-95; ceremonies on, 117-121; description of, 104; explanatory use of, 105
Military Systems, 130
Money, 145-146; distribution, 146; exchange of, 114; inflation of, 146
Motion, 35-37, 65
Mutilations, 118
Multiplication Effects, 36-37, 65

Natural: causation, 19; empirical world, 19; settings, 26
Needs for, 59-60. See functions
Negentropy, 33
Networks, 76-77
Nominalist, 56

Obeisances, 119-120
Observance, 27
Operative: definition of, 75; elaboration of, 78; evolution of, 87-91; militant, 93-95; processes, 69; structures, 69
Original Factors, 53
Organic Analogy, 50-51, 55, 57, 58
Organic Realm, 52-53
Organismic Analogies, 20-21
Oscillation, 40

Paradigm, 25
Parsonian Theory, 14, 15
Patriarchy, 113
Political: authority, 42, 55; dissolution, 125; dialectics, 79-80; institutions, 123-135; leaders, 128-129
Polyandry, 112-123
Polygyny, 112
Polytheism, 139
Population Size, 43-44, 53-55, 55, 67
Positive Philosophy, 16
Power: centralization of, 66-68, 77; decentralization of, 66-68; model of, 80
Preinstitutional, 116
Presents, 118-119
Principles of: centralization of power, 81, 124-135; ceremony, 122; conflict, 134-135; class systems, 134-135; decen-

tralization of power, 82; differentiation, 73-74, 76; dissolution, 41-42; evolution, 34-41; government, 134-135; system size, 73-74; sustaining system, 75
Priests, 76, 139
Productivity, 53-55, 76, 143-146
Promiscuity, 109, 113
Psychology, 52

Realist, 56
Regulatory: axis, 70, 75; differentiation, 75; evolution of, 87-91; functions of, 60; needs, 61; system, 60; structures, 61; types, 93-95
Relativism, 102-103
Religion: bureaucratization of, 140; elements of, 136-137; evolution of, 138-141; functions of, 137; origins of, 137-138; politics of, 137-141
Representative Government, 131-132
Research Problems, 23
Resentments, 81
Resources, 74-78
Rhythms, 65. See oscillation
Science, 18
Segregation, 37, 65
Sentiments, 66, 81, 100
Sexual Equality, 115
Shaman, 139
Size, 57. See principles
Slavery, 149
Socialism, 152-153
Social Darwinism, 11
Social: morphology, 20-27; physiology, 20-27; structure, 28
Society: as a thing, 56; types of, 88-89
Sociology: methods of, 16; science of, 19, 26; theory in, 16
Solidarity, 116-121
Stratification, 132-135. See class systems
Strikes, 151
Structuring, 21, 33, 40, 52, 55, 64-65
Subinstitutional, 117
Super-Organic, 20, 43, 56-58

Sustaining: See operative; axes, 71, 75; differentiation of, 75; functions of, 60; needs of, 61; processes, 62; structures, 60

Synthetic Philosophy, 10, 12, 31, 45-46

System Growth, 58, 60, 64, 68. See size; See principles

Technology, 78, 143-144

Tests, 27

Threat, 81, 82

Titles, 120

Transactions, 76

Trophies, 117-118; unionism, 151-152; universal needs, 59; voluntarism, 58; visits, 119

Wage-Price Spiral, 151

War, 53, 76, 107; effects on government, 125-127; effects on religion, 138-139

World systems, 64

About the Author

Jonathan H. Turner is Professor of Sociology at the University of California at Riverside. He is the author of well over a dozen books on sociological theory, inequality, ethnic relations, and American Society. He has also published in a wide variety of journals in both sociology and anthropology. Currently, he is working on developing abstract theoretical principles of social organization. This work is intended to right what he considers to be a great wrong: the failure to appreciate fully the theoretical and empirical work of Herbert Spencer.

/301S745YT>C1/